INDONESIA

An Amnesty International Report

Amnesty International Publications
1977

First published 1977 by Amnesty International Publications
10 Southampton Street, London WC2E 7HF, England
Copyright Amnesty International Publications
ISBN 0 900058 63 3
AI Index: PUB 77/00/77
Original Language: English
Printed in the United States of America.

SONG OF THE PRISON

Prison-life's a bird alike
Queue-up for maize-rice
Sleepless, your mind troubled
Powerless, your acts bridled

Prison-life's like self-torment
Entering thick, leaving slim
Forced labour and underfed
Still alive but nearly dead.

This song was composed by a prisoner in
Tanggerang Prison, near Jakarta. It is now
known to political prisoners in many
Javanese prisons, and the prisoners continue
to sing it despite attempts by the
authorities to suppress it.

CONTENTS

INTRODUCTION

The situation of political prisoners in Indonesia is profoundly disturbing. With regard to numbers, time-scale, methods used by the government and the history of mass killings and massive arrests, political imprisonment in Indonesia is without parallel today. More than 55,000 political prisoners are distributed throughout the many islands of the Republic of Indonesia; and the correct figure is probably as many as 100,000.

Who are these prisoners? Why are there so many? Why are they transported to permanent penal settlements? Why have so few been tried? Why have vast numbers been held without trial for more than 11 years?

These are the questions with which this report is concerned. Amnesty International has consistently pointed out that the Indonesian Government's policy of political imprisonment amounts to persistent and gross violation of human rights. The facts are simple and terrible.

Tens of thousands of political prisoners in Indonesia are held captive without trial, or used as servants by local military commanders, or exploited as forced labour, or subjected to an archaic policy of transportation to penal colonies. They are ill-treated by the authorities. The majority have now been held prisoner for more than 11 years without trial. Men, women and children are held prisoner, arbitrarily and at the discretion of local military commanders.

The unconstitutional and illegal treatment of the prisoners is illustrated by the political trials of a relatively small number of prisoners. The courts have never been known to acquit a single defendant, and convictions have been based on the merest shreds of evidence. The judges have sentenced prisoners to death or to gross periods of imprisonment. This cynical use of the courts to try prisoners is merely an attempt by the Indonesian Government to present the world with the illusion that they are trying to solve the problem according to established standards of justice.

All Indonesian political prisoners are tightly controlled by the military authorities. The prisoners are at the mercy of local military commanders, who have the power to arrest, interrogate, permit the use of extreme and brutal torture, imprison, use prisoners as servants or forced labour, release and re-arrest them; to act in a completely arbitrary way with regard to people taken captive without charge or trial.

For the prisoners and their families, what happened after an abortive "coup" mounted by a small number of middle-ranking Army officers in 1965 has been a continuing nightmare. First there was the period of fear and uncertainty when the Indonesian Army conducted a nation-wide "inquisition" to destroy what they regarded as left-wing elements in Indonesian society. There were sudden arrests, interrogation and torture, followed by the likelihood of a summons to face summary execution, or the possibility of harsh and interminable imprisonment without charge or trial. All this without any reference to constitutional and legal rights, and carried out completely and arbitrarily at the discretion of local military commanders.

Although there has been growing international concern over the last few years about the plight of political prisoners in Indonesia, governments and ordinary people have been reluctant to express their views because of the complexity of the problem, and because its dimensions often seem incredible. This Amnesty International report describes the situation of Indonesian political prisoners; although the problem is complex, the fundamental issue of Indonesian political imprisonment is simple.

No government has the authority arbitrarily to imprison large numbers of people, unconstitutionally, illegally and contrary to the rule of law. No government should allow political prisoners to be held entirely within a military system of administration which controls all matters concerning political prisoners, and permits local military commanders to exercise complete arbitrary power over political prisoners. No government should transport political prisoners held without trial to permanent penal settlements, or exploit them as forced labour in a daily struggle for survival to produce all their own food and to provision the military garrison guarding them. Military commanders should not be empowered to decide which prisoners are to be released and which held indefinitely; nor empowered to seize the goods and property of prisoners and their families, and to demand large bribes from the latter as the price for releasing their relatives.

A number of political commentators have noted with concern that the "inquisition" in Indonesia has prompted careless speculation elsewhere. When the September 1973 coup in Chile occured, the words "Jakarta, Jakarta" were chalked on to walls, apparently to indicate that some of the participants in the coup were hoping for a repetition of what had taken place in Indonesia. And in Turkey, some right-wing groups have debated whether to follow the "Indonesian example" in order to eradicate the left-wing influence in Turkish politics. In Thailand, following the military coup of October 1976, there has been open speculation among some leading military officers as to whether, if the "Indonesian example" were followed, the country would be able to eradicate left-wing elements for at least a decade. It is in this context that the facts about political imprisonment and its history in Indonesia must be understood. The terrible "inquisition" that was conducted in Indonesia, the mass killings and massive scale of political imprisonment, are a warning of the dangers of such speculation.

Amnesty International considered it its duty over the years to report the facts of Indonesian political imprisonment. This has incurred the displeasure of the Indonesian Government. In a recent speech, General Ali Said, the Indonesian Prosecutor General, was reported to have said that "there cannot be any meeting point between the outlook of the Indonesian Government and Amnesty International. 'For this reason', he said, 'we shall not deal with them'." (*Sinar Harapan*, 6 January 1977).

Amnesty International believes that Indonesian Government policy towards political prisoners is an appropriate and proper subject for international concern and for all who care about human rights. Furthermore, that the international community should make clear representations to President Suharto and his Government in order that they realize that only the immediate and unconditional release of all the prisoners held for so long without trial will provide a just solution.

Amnesty International
June 1977

1

POLITICAL IMPRISONMENT: THE BEGINNING

Indonesia achieved independence from Dutch colonial rule in 1949. The struggle of Indonesian nationalists against colonial rule had been met by severe political repression by the Dutch authorities. From the 1920s, the Dutch colonial government maintained a penal colony at Boven-digoel, in the interior of West Irian, to which political prisoners were transported. At the time of the Japanese invasion during World War II, the Boven-digoel prisoners were moved to Australia, where they were passed off as a dangerous "fifth column". Only a chance meeting between an Australian journalist and one of the prisoners led to the eventual release of the prisoners, many of whom later took part in the war against Japan.

In the years immediately after Independence, there was virtually no political imprisonment in Indonesia. Not until the late 1950s, when there were local rebellions in several regions, were people arrested on a large scale for political reasons. In the early 1960s, most of the several thousand people detained were released under a general amnesty. The Sukarno Government kept a number of political opposition leaders in prison; and journalists and many others who criticized the government policies were arrested and imprisoned.

In the early 1960s, there was an increased polarization in Indonesian politics. The left-wing groupings led by the Communist Party (*Partai Komunis Indonesia*) were opposed by political and military groupings to the right. In October 1965, a small group of left-wing Army officers attempted to destroy the Army leadership by assassinating a number of senior generals. The attempted coup was quickly suppressed by the Army, and President Sukarno's administration was eventually replaced by a military administration. In the aftermath of the attempted coup, the Army carried out a massive and violent purge of people identified as or suspected of being members of the Communist Party, or affiliated to left-wing organizations. In various localities of the Republic, some social and religious groups took advantage of the changed circumstances to take revenge on those they considered responsible for spreading communist doctrine and for having advocated partisan views on issues such as land reform. At that time, as the military took over the national administration, vast numbers of people were taken prisoner.

Of those, more than half a million were killed. This figure was quoted in October 1976 by the head of the Indonesian state security agency in a Dutch television interview. Many independent observers estimate that probably many more than one million people were summarily killed during that period.

Of those who were arrested, but not killed, at least more than half a million were kept in prison. According to Indonesian Government statistics, the authorities had released more than 540 thousand people arrested on suspicion of being communists. Today, there are, throughout Indonesia, tens of thousands of political prisoners held without charge or trial, in connection with the events of 1965. For more than 11 years, the Indonesian Government has maintained its policy of detaining vast numbers of political prisoners without trial.

BACKGROUND TO 1965

In 1957, parliamentary democracy in the Republic of Indonesia was eroded by the promulgation of martial law; later, in 1959, President Sukarno introduced a type of authoritarian rule which was described as "guided democracy". The elected parliament was replaced by an appointed legislature, and the government's executive power was greatly increased. The period of "guided democracy" was associated with Sukarno's distinctive political style and his extrovert foreign policy.

Following the promulgation of martial law in 1957, the Army expanded its influence and became closely involved in political and economic affairs. Many Army officers became government administrators and, in some areas, they wielded unchallenged power. A wide range of Dutch enterprises, nationalized in 1958, were placed under Army control.

The only serious challenge to the growing political power of the Army leadership during this period came from the Communist Party (PKI). The period of "guided democracy", removed the opportunity for the PKI (which in the 1955 elections had polled 16.4% of the votes), to demonstrate its growing strength in national elections. In the 1960s, the party's membership rapidly expanded. By 1965 it exceeded three million. In addition, mass organizations under communist leadership had a combined membership of well over 10 million. The PKI had the largest membership of any communist party outside the Soviet block and the People's Republic of China.

The leadership of the Army and of the PKI worked in a tense and uneasy alliance with President Sukarno, while in some regions there were outbreaks of sharp conflict. In some areas, Communist Party committees were outlawed and their leaders detained by the military. President Sukarno continued to use the Army and the PKI as counterweights against one another.

The PKI criticized the military's management of the economy. In the early 1960s, the PKI aligned itself with China in the Sino-Soviet dispute. Tension increased in 1964 and 1965 when the PKI actively supported unilateral efforts by peasants to expropriate land, in attempts to enforce implementation the 1960 Land Reform Law. Relations between the Army and the PKI became particularly abrasive when the party advocated the creation of a "Fifth Force" of armed peasants and workers to fight against Malaysia alongside regular Indonesian military units. It was then, when there was extreme tension and mutual suspicion, that the attempted coup of 30 September 1965 occurred, and shattered the uneasy alliance between Sukarno, the Army and the PKI.

THE 30 SEPTEMBER AFFAIR

The attempted coup of September 1965 involved mainly middle-ranking military officers led by Lieutenant-Colonel Untung, a battalion commander in the President's Palace Guards. The conspirators intended to destroy the leadership of the Indonesian Army. Six senior generals were kidnapped and assassinated at Halim Airfield, near Jakarta. The coup leaders occupied several important buildings in the capital, where they had the support of Army battalions stationed temporarily in the city.

At that time, members of the pro-PKI mass orgnizations, among others, were being trained for confrontation with Malaysia at Lubang Buaya, the Halim Airfield training ground. The coup leaders had taken a number of political leaders, including the Chairman of the PKI, Aidit, to the Halim base, stating that this was for their personal safety. Just before it was banned, the PKI daily newspaper, *Harian Rakjat,* in its editorial, 2 October, expressed the official view of the Communist Party that the Untung coup was "an internal Army affair".

Those events were interpreted very differently by the Army leadership: in their view, Untung was the chosen instrument of the PKI, and the "coup" was the first step towards setting up a communist government. Under Genral Suharto (as he then was), the Army moved rapidly to crush the attempted coup. Claiming that the entire communist and left-wing movement had been implicated in the coup, the Army raided the Communist Party and left-wing organizations, and there were mass arrests of their leaders and members.

Some of those arrested then were later released in 1966, or shortly after; but to this day many are still in detention. In March 1966,

President Sukarno, who had tried in earlier speeches to stem the tide of persecution and who had initiated investigation into massacres of prisoners, was forced to sign over his executive powers— although not yet his official position— to General Suharto. The day after the order was signed, thirteen of Sukarno's cabinet ministers were arrested and a new cabinet was formed. There followed further mass arrests and this time the net was extended to cover "pro-Sukarno elements" both in the civilian administration and in the armed forces.

In early 1966, a party leader Njono was brought to trial, charged with having enlisted the support of members of pro-PKI mass organizations for the attempted coup. He denied this and other charges, but was found guilty and sentenced to death. Later that year, other trials took place, notably that of Dr Subandrio, who had been President Sukarno's Deputy Prime Minister and Foreign Minister. He too was sentenced to death, although in his case the sentence was not carried out. He is still in prison (see Chapter VI).

The PKI and all its supporting mass organizations were proscribed. The leaders who had avoided capture went underground. At the end of 1966 and the beginning of 1967, there was a further wave of arrests of PKI members who were attempting to revive the party. When the underground movement in Jakarta was effectively crushed, the PKI attempted to create a base in Blitar, in East Java. This was destroyed by the Army.

Some of those detained during the succeeding waves of arrests were alleged to have been involved in illegal activities, but a large number were detained simply because of their past membership of, or former association with the PKI or its mass organizations at a time when these organizations were still legal and when they were prominent in the politics of the Sukarno era.

After the attempted coup, more than half a million people were killed in the ensuing massacres, and more than three-quarters of a million people were arrested and detained. In many cases they were brutally treated. To this day there are numerous untried detainees in prisons throughout the Republic of Indonesia.

For several years after the 1965 events, the Indonesian Government felt justified in holding these prisoners without trial. Till 1972, a number of foreign journalists were allowed to visit political prisons and to report on what they observed. Their reports, without exception, were highly critical of the treatment of the prisoners. Since 1972, the Indonesian authorities have not allowed journalists to visit political prisons, the only exceptions being the conducted visits of Buru by Indonesian journalists accompanied by high ranking

Kopkamtib * officers, and a Dutch television journalist's brief visit in September 1976.

As international concern about Indonesian political prisoners increased, the government took steps to prevent access to political prisons. Consequently, the information available to Amnesty International at present comes from individual confidential sources—people who have managed to evade the government's restriction on access.

The demonstrations and riots centering on the *Malari* Affair in January 1974 were followed by repressive government measures involving imprisonment without trial of large numbers of people and strict press censorship (see Chapter 11). The *Malari* Affair was, among other things, an expression of widespread economic discontent prompting criticism of the failures of the government's development policies. Although eventually, more than two years after the *Malari* Affair, all but three prisoners, who had been tried, were released. *Kopkamtib* surveillance persists in order to prevent criticism of government policies. The government has not lifted its ban on 11 of the most respected newspapers and weeklies.

In recent years, there has been some evolution in government policy statements. Since 1975 "Certificates of Non-Involvement"** were declared no longer necessary prerequisites for access to jobs and education (see also Chapter 9). Because possession of the certificates was denied to the families of prisoners, and to released prisoners, more than half a million people and their dependants were deprived of employment and public education. Despite government statements the "Certificates of Non-Involvement" are still required; consequently many people considered suspect by the government, are effectively penalized and deprived of jobs.

Also in 1975, the government announced that ex-prisoners would have their right to vote restored. This move may have been politically significant; it is generally acknowledged that even in controlled elections, the government faces electoral pressure, especially from the Moslem vote. In the view of some political commentators, the government hoped thereby to draw some secular votes from the hundreds of thousands of released prisoners.

---

* *Kopkamtib.* This is a massive state security apparatus which continues to exist and undertakes surveillance of all aspects of Indonesian political life (see Chapter 3).

** "Certificate of Non-Involvement". A document stating that the holder was innocent of involvement in the events of 1965.

More recently, in December 1976, the government announced an apparently comprehensive release program for the 1965 prisoners (see Chapter 12). However, this program further delays the release of people held without trial for up to 11 years, and involves the transportation of large numbers of prisoners to permanent penal settlements. Moreover, the program is based on official prisoner statistics which greatly underestimate the actual number of prisoners.

**MAIN DETENTION CENTERS HOLDING UNTRIED PRISONERS
HELD IN CONNECTION WITH THE 1965 EVENTS**
Small local prisons are not marked

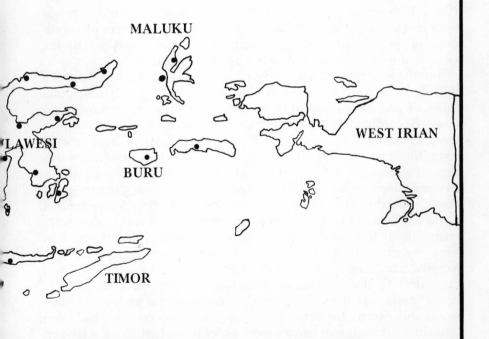

19

PACIFIC OCEAN

MALUKU

LAWESI

BURU

TIMOR

WEST IRIAN

2

POLITICAL IMPRISONMENT: AFTER 1965

The complexities of political imprisonment in Indonesia following the 1965 attempted coup are most easily understood in terms of certain dominant features of government policy and of administrative procedures. Having crushed the attempted coup, the surviving Army leadership sought to eradicate all left-wing elements from the Indonesian body politic. This put at risk a considerable portion of the Indonesian adult population, of whom perhaps one quarter were in some way associated with left-wing organizations or mass movements of one kind or another. There followed what might be described as an "inquisition", whose purpose was to root out all those identifiable as left-wing sympathisers. The inquisition was conducted by the military, whose work was supplemented by religious activists and other vigilante groups which had opposed the increasing strength of left-wing movements in Indonesia during the 1950s and early 1960s. Widespread arrests led to numerous killings, brutal interrogations and subsequent detention in appalling circumstances of thousands of people who were identifiable in some way as having associated with communist or left-wing organizations.

For those prisoners who survived, the Army leadership created a classification system, which distinguished between different categories of people in terms of their association with left-wing organizations. According to this classification, prisoners were divided into those considered to have been directly involved in the attempted coup, those who were indirectly involved, and those who had much looser connections with it. Others who did not fit into these categories were supposed to be released. But it is clear from the history of the prisoners' treatment by the authorities that alleged involvement in the 1965 attempted coup, was only notional; in reality they were held without trial because they were in some way affiliated with left-wing organizations or were thought to have associated with left-wingers. The massive inquisition of these numerous prisoners, from the outset to the present, was undertaken entirely by the military. It was done completely outside the constitutional and legal framework, and except for those relatively few prisoners who had been brought to trial, the detainees were never permitted to see a lawyer, to have their cases examined in any court or in any judicial process. The entire procedure of arrest, interrogation and prolonged detention was undertaken entirely by the military, and all releases were determined by them too.

These then are the dominant features of the Indonesian system of political imprisonment. It was an inquisition carried out by the military against people whom it regarded as its left-wing enemies, and it was almost entirely conducted in an extra-judicial, extra-legal fashion, being essentially an arbitrary procedure decided on by the military.

When the attempted coup was suppressed by the Army, there were successive waves of arrests throughout the Republic. When the prisons were crammed full, temporary detention centers were established. The prisoners included Communist Party members and others who were affiliated to PKI mass organizations, or who were thought generally to have given support to the Communist Party. Others were arrested on suspicion because they had left their homes during the terror that swept the country during the final months of 1965. Others were arrested because of their extremely casual relationships with persons known, or thought to be, communist. Amnesty International's files provide many examples of prisoners who were denounced as communists because they had been involved in a dispute with neighbours, often over question of land ownership, or because they happened to be in a house where someone was arrested, or because they insisted on accompanying a spouse or relative who was being arrested.

The case of Bambang Supeno, an Amnesty International adoptee, illustrates the arbitrariness of arrest. Bambang Supeno, who is blind, deaf and dumb, was arrested in connection with the 1965 events and is detained without trial in Surakarta Prison. The Indonesian authorities have entirely ignored inquiries concerning the charges against him. He may have been detained because of some suspected offence never proven in court, or else because of an administrative error, or as a result of completely arbitrary action on the part of some soldiers. Although the case of Bambang Supeno is striking, there are many prisoners who, like him, are victims of circumstance.

All political arrests made at that time were undertaken by local military commanders, and all legal requirements such as warrants of arrest were totally dispensed with. The military could not cope with the vast numbers taken into custody and recruited people known for their strong opposition to left-wing movements to assist with interrogation. The process of interrogation was rough and arbitrary: on the basis of one word or the pointing of a finger, people were taken away to be killed. Interrogation was intended as revenge and meant to terrorize people. Torture was common and cruel. Estimates of the numbers killed have varied from about 100 thousand to more than a million. In a Dutch television interview in October 1976, the head of the Indonesian state security agency, Admiral Sudomo, gave a definitive estimate: he said that *more than* half a million people were killed following the attempted coup. There can be no doubt about the authority of that estimate, except that the true figure is possibly much higher*.

When "communist suspects" were arrested, their relatives and friends were afraid to visit them because of the real danger that they too would be arrested. Former associates of such prisoners were afraid to speak out for them. Prisoners were moved from camp to camp and eventually into more permanent, but inadequate, prisons. The numbers were so vast and involved chaotic transportation of prisoners and so many people died in detention, that the administration was incapable of keeping adequate records. Families of prisoners themselves often had to move because of desperate circumstances or local hostility. Many prisoners vanished without trace, and their families assumed they were dead.

Because of the massive scale of arrests, virtually every Indonesian now over the age of 30 can recall at least one occasion in the period following the attempted coup, when someone known to him or her was taken away. This might have been some close or distant relative, a school-mate or a university friend, a colleague or a neighbour. At that time, caution and obligations to their own dependants deterred them from making appeals on behalf of the prisoners. It was dangerous to be known to be helping a prisoner's family. As they were not in a position to help, nor even to discuss the position of individual prisoners, virtually every free person, including lawyers, avoided the question of political imprisonment. In a sense, the prisoners were forgotten by their own communities.

Even now, the plight of individual prisoners, or of prisoners generally, is a topic to be avoided, except when talking to the most intimate friends. People are still being arrested on the suspicion of being communist, or because they are suspected of some degree of involvement in the 1965 abortive coup. Numerous people are still being purged from jobs in government departments and agencies, and from

* The grim events of 1965 and 1966 are described in a number of autobiographical short stories, by young Moslem men who describe how they were involved in the capture of communist suspects, assisted in interrogation and in the killing of prisoners. Ten of these short stories are translated by Harry Aveling in *GESTAPU: Indonesian Short Stories of the Abortive Communist Coup of 30 September 1965*, South East Asian Studies Working Paper No.6, University of Hawaii, 1975.

the armed forces, for allegedly having some connection with the PKI.

The events of the past decade have had increasingly disastrous repercussions on the prisoners' families. Less than 15% of all prisoners have received any visit from friends and relatives; and less than 3% are receiving regular visits from their relatives. Because of the widespread prejudice against prisoners and their families, and because it is difficult for married women to find work in Indonesian society, the pressure on the wives of prisoners has been such that out of the total population of married male prisoners, more than half have been divorced by their wives. Of those prisoners who are in the penal colony of Buru Island, more than three-quarters of the married male prisoners have been divorced by their wives. The same high statistic applies to prisons such as Cipinang, in Jakarta.

To summarize, the effects of the "inquisition" can be understood in crude statistical terms. In 1965, out of a total population of perhaps 120 million, there was an adult population of possibly 40 million. Of those adults, 10 million—that is, one-quarter of the adult population—were members of, or in some way connected with, mass organizations under Communist Party leadership. Those 10 million people were threatened by the inquisition. In the aftermath of the 1965 events, more than half a million were killed, and about one million people arrested, interrogated and detained. Many of them are still prisoners, held without trial after more than 11 years in detention. In mid-1977, they probably total as many as 100 thousand.

Mere statistics alone do not adequately describe the terrible experience of many people in the aftermath of the 1965 events. The following two accounts illustrate the arbitrariness and terror experienced by many people during that period. The first account is that of a prisoner, and the second of a person who became an inquisitor.

The prisoner, who cannot be named, was arrested in early 1966. Initially his wife was afraid to make inquiries about him for fear she too were arrested. Later, she searched for him and failed to find him. The prisoner could not contact his family. The wife could not support her children and was forced to abandon their family home. She assumed her husband was dead.

One of their children was six years old when his father was taken away. He was especially devoted to his father. He became emotionally disturbed and obsessive about finding his father, and walked the streets asking strangers whether they had seen him. In early 1974, eight years after his father's arrest, he had grown into a boy of 14 who was mentally retarded, still obsessive and wandering from home in search of his father, showing passing strangers an old photograph. One day in early 1974, he walked by Salemba Prison in Jakarta and showed the photograph to a passing prison official. The boy thus found his father, after eight years. He was a prisoner in Salemba, where he had eventually been transferred.

The second account is that of an Indonesian writer who published an autobiographical short story using the pseudonym of Usamah.* Usamah was fearful of a communist victory in the 1965 attempted coup. He described how he became a civilian member of an interrogation team, and on several occasions had to interrogate his own friends. The first was a woman schoolteacher, who during interrogation indicated that she knew him. Anxious that this should not be misinterpreted by the guards, he "was forced to order them to 'torture the bitch' ". She was tortured, and later signed a confession.

The second case involved Usamah's former family doctor:

"I suggested to my superior that he appoint someone more scientifically minded to work on the doctor. The commander misunderstood me and sent a torturer. I watched the familiar gangland scene without being able to do anything to stop it. He screamed for mercy as the blows of the belt buckle rained down on him."

Later, Usamah had to interrogate another prisoner, a girl called Sri, who was a former classmate. He had to identify her and 13 other prisoners, and get them taken away by soldiers to be killed. Usamah identified Sri. He also identified Mrs Y, the schoolteacher he had previously interrogated, who was also on the list. The soldiers took the prisoners to Mojo, a village in the west of Solo. They shouted abuse at the prisoners, and "their shouts grew more hysterical and reverberated throughout the village as the 14 prisoners walked slowly to the river's edge. Sri cried as soon as she was taken off the truck. Mrs Y was calm, although her face was as bitter as a dry lemon. They were lined up in rows at the steep bank of the river. I can still hear them weeping. . .".

These two accounts illustrate many of the common features of the inquisition: arrest, extremely brutal interrogation, arbitrary selection of people for killing by soldiers and anti-communist militants, arbitrary detention of people without trial carried out in such a way

---

* The article was first published in August 1969 in the Indonesian journal, *Horison*, and was subsequently re-published in the prestigious Jakarta paper, *Indonesia Raya*, which was banned in 1974. It is now available in English translation in Harry Aveling, *GESTAPU (Ibid.)*.

that prisoners still cannot be found by their families even after many years.

3

ADMINISTRATIVE CONTROL OF PRISONERS

The Army had rallied under the leadership of General Suharto to crush the attempted coup and to destroy its left-wing enemies. General Suharto, on 10 October 1965 set up a "Command for the Restoration of Security and Order", with himself as the Commander. The Command, known as *Kopkamtib,* has wide powers to investigate and control political activity in the Republic. The decrees and orders issued by *Kopkamtib* empower Army officers to arrest people for political reasons. To fulfil its tasks, *Kopkamtib* has at its disposal all the resources of the Army. The Command interrogates all arrested persons; in addition, it summons suspects to its centers for interrogation. *Kopkamtib* headquarters are in the same complex of buildings in Jakarta as the Ministry of Defence.

Arrest, interrogation, detention and classification are carried out by Army officers who derive their authority from *Kopkamtib.* Civilian officials, law officers, lawyers and the judiciary are entirely excluded from this process. Political prisoners are not allowed to consult lawyers, nor may they appeal to the court against wrongful detention. It is not until prisoners are brought to trial that their cases are transferred from *Kopkamtib* to the Office of the Prosecutor General, and it is not until then that civilian officials have access to their files. Only when the prisoners actually go on trial do they have the opportunity of consulting a lawyer, who is often appointed by the court.

Immediately after the 1965 attempted coup, it was standard practice for *Kopkamtib,* and Army officers acting under its authority to inflict extremely brutal torture when interrogating prisoners. This continued for several years, until gradually the use of torture in interrogation became less systematic. By 1970, those prisoners who had been detained for several years were less likely to be tortured; and whether a particular prisoner was tortured depended on the attitudes of the interrogating officers, and the practice at that particular interrogation center.

Today, torture is still used in the interrogation centers that exist in all the large towns throughout the Republic. Large cities have several interrogation centers. In Jakarta, for example, there are interrogation centers in Jalan Tanah Abang, Gunung Sahari and Kebayoran Lama. The center at Jalan Tanah Abang has been particularly notorious for its use of torture.

Political prisoners can be kept in interrogation centers for varying periods of up to several years, and because they are under interrogation they are not allowed visitors. Quite often prisoners in regular political detention centers also are interrogated. It is common for prisoners who have been detained for more than 10 years to be subjected to renewed interrogation and they may be transferred to an interrogation center for this purpose.

Although 11 years have passed since the 1965 events, people are still often arrested on suspicion of past association with the banned organizations. Of these, the most unfortunate are officers and men serving in the armed forces who are suspected of some past affiliation with left-wing organizations, and are detained in special interrogation centers maintained by military units, where extremely brutal torture is usual (the Air Force detention center in Jakarta is particularly notorious).

Others as well as suspected communists are exposed to the *Kopkamtib* system. Although the people arrested and detained in connection with the *Malari* Affair of January 1974 were not regarded by the authorities as communists and were not tortured, many of them faced severe and prolonged interrogation (see Chapter 11). Journalists were summoned for interrogation and questioned about articles they had written. The distinguished former ambassador to the United States, Mr Soedjatmoko, was interrogated for three weeks for suspected involvement in the events of January 1974.

The various ways in which the state security system and control of prisoners operates is increasingly extreme and all-pervasive. The arbitrary powers available to *Kopkamtib*; the total military control in all matters relating to political arrest, interrogation and imprisonment, to the exclusion of civilian, judicial, and ordinary law-enforcement officials; the arbitrary nature of arrest, detention and classification, with denial of the right to appeal to the courts or to any other authority; the lack of supervision and the total absence of independent checks on the exercise of the almost unlimited powers of individual military officers; the use of torture; all these factors created an overwhelming structure of intimidation and repression. When Indonesian citizens are taken prisoner on suspicion of political deviations, they are at the mercy of their interrogators, who may treat them as they please.

CLASSIFICATION OF PRISONERS

General Suharto relinquished his position as Commander of *Kopkamtib* when he became President of the Republic. But following the student demonstrations of January 1974, he again appointed himself Commander of *Kopkamtib,* a position he still holds, indicating the importance he attaches to the state security agency. The workings of *Kopkamtib* are particularly important to political prisoners affecting their status and their prospects of release. This stems from *Kopkamtib's* authority to classify prisoners by a process involving different military units, and especially their "screening teams" which examine the prisoners' files.

The official basis of *Kopkamtib's* authority to classify prisoners is derived from the presidential instruction signed on President Sukarno's behalf by General Suharto and issued in May 1966. That decree defined three levels of "involvement" in the 1965 events. Under President Suharto, the 1966 presidential instruction was amended in 1969 to its present form currently applicable to all political prisoners held in connection with the 1965 events. The decree represents the Government's view of the varying degrees of alleged culpability of different categories of prisoners, and defines Government policy towards each category (see Appendix I).

This presidential instruction, as it stands and without further elaboration, has provided the sole basis for administrative action against more than one million people. Every Indonesian citizen who has been suspected of left-wing affiliation or opinions, fell into one or other of the vague categories defined in the presidential instruction. The purpose of interrogation and screening was to decide if and how a prisoner fitted into one of the categories listed in the decree.

These instructions to *Kopkamtib* were intended to be extraordinarily wide-ranging. They were supposed to apply not only to those who were suspected of having played an active part in the 1965 attempted coup, but also to those alleged to have known about it and to have "assumed an attitude" which suggested they had been sympathetic to it. It applied also to those who belonged to organizations before they were proscribed in 1966. Most imprecise of all, they were supposed to apply to "those who have shown sympathy for the PKI in their attitudes and actions".

The 1969 instructions were specifically intended to "improve" the screening of people serving in civilian government departments and in military units. Special screening teams employing large numbers of army officers operate in every region under the supervision of the central screening office in Jakarta. The amended 1969 instructions provided the basis for a major campaign which involved screening the staff of all departments and units, and this process was again initiated in 1974. There were many reports in 1974 and

1975 of regional and local departments, such as post offices, medical and educational institutions, being purged of large numbers of suspects. In some cities, entire government offices lost more than half their personnel following the screening of the staff.

The number purged was so great that some observers believe political screening was used partly to disguise rationalization of the administration, thereby eliminating the chronic problem of over-staffing in government departments. There appear to have been other reasons too, such as victimization and the continuing policy of punishment and stigmatization on the slenderest of evidence. Most of the victims of this general screening of people, non-prisoners found themselves put in one of the C sub-categories. In 1969 and 1970, C category people were still being arrested. By 1974 and 1975, they were supposed to have been released, and so most of those who were subject to the later screening did not end up as prisoners. However, people continued to be arrested as category A or B prisoners, or as prisoners of indeterminate category until the screening teams had completed their assessment of the individual cases concerned. Today, there are still category C prisoners and the authorities justify their continued imprisonment by maintaining that they have been re-categorized into category B.

Screening was aimed particularly at the "mass organizations" which were proscribed in 1966. These were listed in a presidential decision issued in May of that year, signed by General Suharto on behalf of President Sukarno. In addition to all the PKI committees, from the Central Committee down to the village committees, the list included 26 mass organizations and 23 educational institutions. It included in the case of the trade union federation *SOBSI* a sub-list of 62 trade unions, and *Baperki,* an organization of Indonesian citizens of Chinese ethnic origin, plus a sub-list comprising two mass organizations and the *Baperki*-run *Res Publica* University. The combined membership in 1965 of these organizations was estimated to be about twenty million. Allowing for double counts in the case of persons belonging to more than one organization and excluding those who were virtually inactive, the actual figure would probably have been about half this total. For the purposes of screening and arrest, the deciding factor was nominal rather than active membership. It is therefore no exaggeration to say that the measures taken by the Government and the Army: the arrests, dishonourable dismissals and decrees of general ineligibility to obtain employment or education have, in some way, affected about ten million people plus the members of their families. Although the mass arrests that took place and still continue are in the main directed at left wingers, their followers or supporters, many Indonesians, especially members of the armed forces, were also arrested for being "Sukarno-ists", since it was the continuing aim of President Suharto's "New Order" to condemn policies followed by President Sukarno in the period before September 1965.

Because the screening and classifying process did not in any way involve legal and judicial procedures, the categories to which prisoners were assigned by their military interrogators could not be questioned in any way. The prisoners are not informed of the category into which they have been placed, even though prison commanders keep lists of prisoners divided into the different categories. When prisoners are awaiting classification as categories A, B or C, they are placed in category X. This residual category is also used for those who are being re-classified—a haphazard process which can raise or lower a prisoner's status.

The formal classification system, although vague, nonetheless affected prisoners in a very direct way. Those in category A were deemed to have been "directly involved" in the 1965 events. These prisoners are supposed to be brought to trial, but the proceedings have been extremely slow: an average of less than one hundred prisoners a year having been tried. Then there are those in category B, deemed to have been "indirectly involved", whom the Government never intended to bring to trial but were being held indefinitely without trial. Category C, with its sub-categories, comprised those whose "involvement" in the 1965 events was presumed merely on the basis that "indications exist" or "may reasonably be assumed".

Most Indonesian political prisoners can only speculate about the category to which they have been assigned. They know that they have been classified as category A when they have been brought to trial; and they know they have been assigned to one of the sub-categories of category C when they are released. Occasionally, there are prisoners (such as those on the island of Buru, to which only category B prisoners are transported) who are reasonably certain what category they are in (see Chapter 4).

The general effect of the presidential decree about classification of prisoners rendered the entire process of political imprisonment a completely extra-legal, military monopoly. A vast military bureaucracy, quite arbitrary and unchallenged, made decisions affecting individual prisoners.

4

CLASSIFICATION AND NUMBERS

The classification system allows local military commanders and their staff wide discretionary powers to classify particular prisoners. For the prisoners themselves, this arbitrary classification has far-reaching consequences. It may mean that the prisoner will theoretically face the prospect of a trial; it may mean that the prisoner faces the prospect of indefinite detention without trial; it may mean that the prisoner will be released. The implications for a prisoner of being placed in one or other of the categories are examined in this chapter.

CATEGORY A

The Indonesian authorities regard category A prisoners as those whom they consider were directly involved in the 1965 abortive coup. This is the only group of prisoners whom the Government has stated it intends to bring to trial. Over the years, official statements have been made about the number of prisoners in category A:

— in September 1971, General Sugih Arto, then Prosecutor General, told foreign journalists that there were about 5,000 category A prisoners;

— in February 1972, General Sumitro, then Deputy-Commander of *Kopkamtib*, told journalists that there were 2,494 category A prisoners;

— in October 1973, General Ali Murtopo, deputy chief of the state intelligence agency and at that time a senior advisor to the President, told members of Amnesty International in Australia that there were 2,457 category A prisoners;

— in February 1976, Amnesty International was informed that the official *Kopkamtib* figure for category A prisoners was 1,745.

There have been a number of official statements about the Government's intention to bring category A prisoners to trial. In July 1974, the head of the Jakarta Prosecutor's Office, Soegiro Tjokrodidjojo, stated that 800 of the category A prisoners had been tried since 1965 (*Indonesian Times*, 26 July 1974). In February 1976, Amnesty International received the official *Kopkamtib* estimate that a further 745 category A prisoners were to be put on trial, and that an estimated 200 cases would be tried annually. Moreover, it was stated that "the other 1,000 (category A prisoners) would be dealt with through re-classification".

Indonesian Government officials are prepared to concede that the rate at which category A prisoners have been brought to trial has been extremely slow. On average annually, less than a hundred have been tried since 1965. Despite repeated government statements that they intend to speed up the rate of category A trials, there has been no significant change in the annual number. At this rate, there will still be category A prisoners pending trial 15 years hence; which will mean that some category A detainees will have to spend a total of 25 years in prison before coming to trial. The Indonesian Government has been constantly criticized for the slow rate of trials of category A prisoners, as in effect it means many of the latter cannot expect to be tried within their lifetimes. This has prompted more recent official statements which try to avoid the issue. Hence, the *Kopkamtib* estimate that "the other 1,000 (category A prisoners) will be dealt with through re-classification", which apparently means that 1,000 category A prisoners will be re-classified as category B. And on 1 December 1976, the government announced that all category A prisoners "will certainly be tried in our courts of justice". Despite such assurances, it must be pointed out that government promises made over several years that category A prisoners would be brought to trial expeditiously have not led to any significant improvements.

Of the hundreds of thousands of prisoners arrested in connection with the 1965 events, a mere fraction have come to trial in 11 years. Besides, the conduct of trials is unsatisfactory (see Chapter 6).

CATEGORY B

This category, by definition, includes not only those who had "assumed an attitude" which implied support for the attempted coup, but includes also those who were leaders and members of the PKI or related mass organizations. They are deemed to have been involved "indirectly" in the attempted coup. The Indonesian authorities have maintained that they would not put the category B prisoners on trial because there was insufficient evidence against them, even though the authorities continued to imprison them for alleged indirect involvement. The official view was that category B prisoners were a danger to security and public order. It was government policy to detain category B prisoners until they had abandoned their communist ideology and adopted the Indonesian principles of *Panca Sila*.* Although the Government repeatedly stressed the importance of "ideological rehabilitation" of category B prisoners, yet they never specified what they meant by an adequate process of rehabilitation, nor did they initiate programs to achieve the prisoners' rehabilitation. The Government never defined which criteria would indicate that "ideological rehabilitation" had been sufficient to warrant release.

Until 1975, less than five category B prisoners are known to have been released. In January 1975, nine prisoners known to be in category B were released. The fact that, after ten years, there were extremely few category B prisoners released revealed the emptiness of the government's policy based on the notion of "ideological rehabilitation".

In some ways, the plight of the category B prisoners arises from the most extreme aspects of the Indonesian Government's policy towards prisoners generally. Compare them, for example, with category A prisoners, who at least are promised trials even though the trial process is draconian and excessively slow; the latter at least face the prospect of release after serving specific sentences. And category C prisoners have been the subject of repeated government assurances that they would all be released, or else that they had been released. But nothing was known about category B prisoners, except that the Government intended to hold them indefinitely without trial, until the new programme of 1 December 1976 was announced.

In 1969 the Government transferred 10,000 prisoners from Java to penal camps on Buru Island; this scheme being intended to be a permanent solution to the problem of category B prisoners. It has been government policy that these prisoners should not leave Buru (see Chapter 9).

Until late 1976, Government policy as regards category B prisoners in no way suggested there was any possibility, even in the distant future, of all category B prisoners being released. Amnesty International is unaware of a single policy statement made before 1976, indicating that sometime in the future category B prisoners would not be a permanent feature of Indonesian society.

There was a remarkable change in government policy statements on 1 December 1976, when the head of the Indonesian state security agency announced plans to release and/or "transmigrate"* all category B detainees (see Appendix II, for Admiral Sudomo's statement).

The new government program announced by Admiral Sudomo on

---

* *Panca Sila*: these are the five "pillars" of the Indonesian State: belief in one God, nationalism, humanitarianism, democracy and social justice.

1 December 1976 was avowedly for the "release of the category B detainees" over a period of three years. During 1977 and 1978, 10,000 of these prisoners are to be released each year. In 1979, the remainder are to be released.

The 1 December program indicates significant progress in the Indonesian Government's attitude towards the prisoners. It was the very first time the Government had ever stated that all category B prisoners *could* be released, and that the Government intended to release all these prisoners. However, the Government's statement cannot be accepted at face value. Admiral Sudomo talked about releasing category B prisoners, but simultaneously announced the Government's intention to transport them to "transmigration centers in Sumatra, Kalimantan, Sulawesi and other places". Prisoners especially from Java are to be "transmigrated" to the penal island of Buru and other islands. "Release" of this kind cannot be thought of in the generally accepted sense, since the prisoners are virtually banished from their homes, in some cases to penal settlements more than 1,000 kilometers away from their families and home areas, to which they are not allowed to return. For those compulsorily transported to Buru or equivalent penal colonies, the so-called "releases" in fact amount to a fate worse than their present imprisonment without trial.

From what is known of the Government's program on Buru Island, Amnesty International has consistently and vigorously criticized the Indonesian Government for its schemes to "transmigrate" prisoners to penal colonies (see Chapter 9). The Indonesian Government has maintained that this "transmigration" of prisoners is "in accordance with the guidelines on national transmigration as set out in the second Five Year National Development Program". Amnesty International finds the Indonesian Government's explanation completely unacceptable and has pointed out that such policy and practice contravenes basic internationally-accepted standards of human rights. Transportation to indefinite detention in a penal colony cannot be interpreted as equivalent to release to ordinary life.* Unlike ordinary Indonesian citizens, who choose to be "transmigrated", the prisoners cannot choose whether to be "transmigrated" rather than allowed to return to their families.

The reasons given by the Indonesian Government for their policy of "transmigration", delaying for a further three years the release

---

* Transmigration: Ostensibly resettlement in accordance with the Government's intention to even out the distribution of population in the major islands. But the effect for political prisoners is virtually compulsory exile from their home regions and families.

of people whom it considers *can* be released, are based on arguments about unemployment in Indonesia. Admiral Sudomo said: "There must be sufficient employment opportunities for them, since unemployment would create fertile ground for all kinds of acts contrary to law, and this in itself would pose a threat to the national security, particularly to law and order."

National unemployment and underemployment in Indonesia is not a phenomenon for which prisoners can be blamed. The Government arguments about unemployment, used to justify the more than three year delay over releasing prisoners and the need to "transmigrate" them, is completely unacceptable, since these arguments apply to tens of thousands of prisoners, many of whom have been held for more than 11 years without trial and whose presumed guilt has never been established. National unemployment is a problem for the Government to solve in other ways, and category B prisoners should be released immediately. Amnesty International is in no doubt that the prisoners' greatest fear is compulsory "transmigration". They want to be released.

Amnesty International believes that only when the Indonesian Government implements prompt release of all category B prisoners, without qualification and without schemes to "transmigrate" them to Buru and other places, will the prisoners' position really change.

As regards the number of category B prisoners currently held, the Government's statistics have been confusing and misleading:

— in November 1970, Sean MacBride (then Chairman of Amnesty International's Executive Committee, also Nobel laureate), was told by General Sudharmono that there were 15,000 category B prisoners;

— in February 1972, General Sumitro told journalists that there were 16,076 category B prisoners;

— an article in the Indonesian newspaper *Merdeka* on 16 September 1974 quoted official statistics, that there were 27,000 category B prisoners, of whom 10,000 were on Buru and the remainder in various prisons in Java;

— official *Kopkamtib* figures, communicated to Amnesty International in February 1976, gave the total number of category B prisoners at that time as 29,480. (The official breakdown of the total number of category B prisoners is given in the following table).

---

* Transportation: Compare for example, the practice of the British in the 19th century of transporting criminal prisoners to its Australian Colony.

Total of the category B detainees
and those already released, according to *Kopkamtib*
(February 1976)

No.	Regions	Detained	Released
1	Aceh	32	—
2	North Sumatra	1,728	62
3	West Sumatra/Riau	2,810	—
4	South Sumatra	588	—
5	Jakarta Raya	981	102
6	West Java	1,124	156
7	Central Java/Yogyakarta	1,799	828
8	East Java	1,404	47
9	East Borneo	1,172	—
10	South/Central Borneo	274	—
11	West Borneo	593	34
12	North/Central Celebes	1,515	10
13	South/Southeast Celebes	422	—
14	Moluccas	710	19
15	East Indonesia	363	51
16	Irian Jaya	24	—
17	Plantungan	380	—
18	Nusa Kambangan	2,379	—
19	Buru Island	11,085	—
20	Central Interrogative Team	87	—
Total		29,470	1,309

These *Kopkamtib* statistics are demonstrably false. To take the example of just one region—Central Java—the actual number of category B prisoners detained in that region is at least twice the *Kopkamtib* total. The *Kopkamtib* figure, although received by Amnesty International in February 1976, relates to the situation prevailing in 1975. It was in 1975 that the government announced that they had released 1,309 category B prisoners, which is the total figure of those released according to the *Kopkamtib* statistics. The information available to Amnesty International about the number of prisoners in Central Java at that time gave a very different picture from that of the *Kopkamtib* statistics.

The official statistics for Central Java are confusing because figures for two major detention centers in that region (Plantungan and Nusa kambangan) are given separately from the Central Java statistics. Therefore, the official statistic items numbered 7, 17 and 18 are combined to give a total number of category B prisoners in Central Java of 4,558, plus 828 released, giving an overall total of 5,386.

According to equivalent statistics available to Amnesty International, there were in the known main detention centers of Central Java, at that time, the following numbers of prisoners:

Nusa kambangan	4,800
Plantungan	420
Purwokerto	750
Pekalongan	490
Bulu	120
Mlaten	680
Ambarawa	910
Magelang	180
Jogjakarta	590
Surakarta	470
Pati	460
Total	9,870

The total number of prisoners in the known main detention centers in Central Java, according to Amnesty International information, totalled 9,870.

The official *Kopkamtib* statistics related only to category B prisoners, and separate figures were given for category A prisoners, which, according to *Kopkamtib*, totalled 1,745. The majority of the category A prisoners were detained in the prisons near the capital, Jakarta, in West Java. Even allowing for the fact that a number of category A prisoners are included in the Amnesty International figures given above, the real number of prisoners in this category in just the two regions of East Java and Central Java cannot be more than a few hundred. (Moreover, Government statistics given from 1974 onwards have consistently excluded category C prisoners, and the Amnesty International figures previously mentioned also do not include category C prisoners.)

The discrepancy between official *Kopkamtib* statistics and the real situation in Central Java is considerable. Taking into account only the main detention centers in Central Java, at the end of 1974 there were at least 4,000 more prisoners than the official figure of 5,376. When remaining detention centers in the other cities and towns of Central Java are taken into consideration, the actual numbers of category B prisoners in Central Java must be considerably higher. Amnesty International consider the official *Kopkamtib* figures amount to no more than about half the actual totals. The actual numbers are considerably more than twice the total admitted by *Kopkamtib*.

It is because of such serious discrepancies that the *Kopkamtib* figure of 29,470 category B prisoners in detention during 1975 cannot be considered accurate. Claims by the Indonesian authorities that they hold less than 30,000 category B prisoners conceal the truth.

While the official breakdown of the category B statistics reveals that political prisoners are to be found throughout the Republic, the figures themselves are a serious underestimate of the actual numbers of category B prisoners being held. At the very least, the actual number exceeds the official total of 29,470 by a minimum of 30,000 more prisoners not accounted for in the official statistics.

CATEGORY C

Category C comprises "persons of whom indications exist or who may reasonably be assumed to have been directly or indirectly involved" in the 1965 attempted coup. In practice, category C is divided into the following three sub-categories:

— category C-1. This sub-category resembles category B and includes persons whom the authorities consider to have been involved in the coup to a lesser degree than those in category B;

— category C-2. This includes those who were members of the mass organizations affiliated with the PKI or other mass organizations "based on the same principles" as the PKI;

— category C-3. This includes those who have "shown sympathy for the PKI by their attitudes and actions".

The sub-categories C-2 and C-3 apply also to people who are not prisoners but who may have been arrested for interrogation and detention and were subsequently released. The people in these two sub-categories have been subjected to the mass screening and purges (see Chapter 3).

The Indonesian Government has made particularly misleading

statements concerning category C prisoners:

- in November 1970, Sean MacBride was told by General Sugih Arto, then Prosecutor General, that government policy as regard category C prisoners was that they should eventually be released; that the original target had been late 1969 or early 1970, and that it was government policy to release all the category C prisoners by the end of 1971;

- General Sudharmono, then Secretary of the State Secretariat, told Sean MacBride in November 1970 that there were at that time 25,000 category C prisoners;

- in August 1971, General Sugih Arto stated that there were 50,000 category C prisoners, all of whom would be freed before the end of the year. In a speech to foreign journalists in September 1971, he said that the Indonesian Government was releasing category C prisoners and hoped not to have a single one left by the end of that year;

- in October 1971, General Marpaung, speaking for the Minister of Defence and Security, said that there were 3,112 category C prisoners;

- in January 1972, President Suharto announced that "all 22,000 category C prisoners" had been released;

- in February 1972, General Sumitro, then head of *Kopkamtib*, told journalists that there were no longer any category C prisoners in detention;

- in August 1972, and again in March 1973, President Suharto stated that all category C prisoners had been released and had been returned to normal life;

- in October 1973, the figures for political prisoners given by General Ali Murtopo to members of Amnesty International in Australia included no category C prisoners;

- a Dutch parliamentary mission which visited Indonesia in September 1974 was told by Mr Ali Said, the Prosecutor General, that the category C prisoners had *not* all been released. He said the decision had been made in principle to release these prisoners before 1972, but the power to decide on the phasing of these releases had been left to regional military commanders and these commanders exercised their powers in different ways. According to the Prosecutor General, "It is quite possible that one territory might have reached its target before another, but it is certain that ultimately in 1975 everyone must have solved this problem".

In January and in August 1972, and again in March 1973, President Suharto declared that all category C prisoners had been released. Other leading Indonesian generals claimed that there were no longer any category C prisoners in detention. In September 1974, the Prosecutor General revealed that there were an undisclosed number of category C prisoners in detention.

It is clear that, despite assurances by the President, and by the then Prosecutor General, there are still large numbers of category C prisoners in detention throughout Indonesia; and there is no doubt that the regional military commanders with "the power to decide on the phasing of these releases" have "exercised their power in different ways".

For example, on 5 October 1976, long after the deadline when it was "certain that ultimately in 1975 everyone must have solved this problem", the *Indonesian Times*, published in Jakarta, reported that the military commander of the Merdeka Division, Brigadier General Edi Sugarto, the official responsible for the maintenance of security in Manado, had released a group of 15 prisoners. Of these, six were category C. (The remaining nine prisoners were category B, and were described as having been "released" by changing their "status" to "city or house arrest".)

Official government estimates of the total prisoner population since 1972 have entirely ignored the category C prisoners, thereby giving a false impression of the real total number of all categories of prisoners. Again, to take only one recent example, the Indonesian Foreign Minister, Mr Adam Malik, when questioned by European parliamentarians in the debate following his speech to the Council of Europe at Strasbourg in April 1975, insisted that the total of prisoners in all categories in Indonesia was 20,000. The figure given by the Indonesian Foreign Minister was demonstrably false, since it failed even to account for all the prisoners in category B, and was clearly intended to give the misleading impression that all category C prisoners had been released.

5

OVERALL DIMENSIONS OF IMPRISONMENT

When the Indonesian Foreign Minister, Adam Malik, replied to questions about political detention in Indonesia at the Parliamentary Assembly of the Council of Europe in the session of 22 April 1975, he indicated the scale of imprisonment in Indonesia:

> "Immediately after the abortive coup in 1965, we began in 1966 to seize people for interrogation who had been connected with the coup. The number at that time was about 600,000. On the basis of our prevailing laws, our religious conscience and our humanitarian conscience, we immediately began to discover whether people were guilty or not. In that process, from a total of 600,000 there are now only about 20,000 left, and they fall into various categories. These people will be brought to trial. Those who already have been found not guilty have been released. As others are found not guilty, they too will be released."

It was noted in the previous chapter that the Indonesian Foreign Minister's claim that "there are now only about 20,000 left", is demonstrably false. Moreover, it has never been Indonesian government policy that all those prisoners remaining "will be brought to trial".

The Foreign Minister's statement about the overall numbers detained since 1965, giving the figure of 600,000, relates to arrests in the years immediately following 1965. His figures should be compared with those of Admiral Sudomo, Chief of Staff of *Kopkamtib,* who said in an interview with a Dutch television journalist that after the coup, 750,000 people were arrested. (*Televisie Radio Omroep Stichting,* 9 October 1976).

The official figures of 600,000 or 750,000 arrested, do not include the number who were killed. In the same television interview, Admiral Sudomo said that half a million "communists" were killed. In another interview with the same journalist, quoted in the Dutch newspaper *De Telegraaf* (11 June 1976), Admiral Sudomo said, "Well, there were between 450,000 and 500,000 [alleged communists killed after the attempted coup], but those had not been killed by the military forces. This was revenge from the people of Java and Sumatra, mostly Islamic youngsters. If the communists had come to power it would have been much worse".

The official figures also do not take account of the pattern of arrest and detention that has continued long after the immediate aftermath of the abortive coup. The former Indonesian Prosecutor General, General Sugih Arto, explained to a gathering of foreign journalists in Jakarta in September 1971, "It is impossible to say exactly how many political prisoners there are. It is a floating rate, like the Japanese yen vis-à-vis the dollar". He further explained, "The thing is that local commanders have the power to arrest and interrogate any person under suspicion of being a threat to national security. These people can be held for an unlimited period of time. It is not always compulsory to report such security arrests to the central command in Jakarta".

In October 1972, a senior officer of *Kopkamtib* said that the number of political prisoners being held had its "ups and downs". This was because "On the very day we release or sentence someone, we shall probably be arresting others".

All available information from Indonesia confirms the official statements that arrests continued to be made of people suspected of involvement in the 1965 events. Because of the so-called "floating rate" in the number of prisoners, it is important to know what the actual scale of imprisonment is at any one time, rather than accept the artificial and illusory precision of official figures. Being aware of this problem, Amnesty International rounds off figures to the relevant tens of thousands.

The official figures of 600,000 and 750,000 people arrested and imprisoned, should be considered also in relation to the Indonesian Government's claims about releases. One statement about releases was issued by the Indonesian Embassy in London on 14 November 1972: the statistics released then were described as official statistics originating from the Prosecutor General's Office and the Department of Security and Defence about the number of political prisoners released each year from 1966 to 1972:

Year	Number of prisoners released
1966	146,200
1967	94,000
1968	86,000
1969	61,000
1970	49,000
1971	35,000
1972	30,000
Total	501,200

After 1972, official overall statistics were no longer made available. The only figures about releases are those relating only to category B prisoners, 1,309 of whom the Government claimed to have released by the end of December 1975, and 2,500 were declared released on 1 December 1976.

Note that the above listed figures add up to 501,200. These figures were given at a time when the Government claimed that it had released all category C prisoners, and the figures issued were intended by the Government to bear out this claim. In other words, by November 1972, when the Indonesian Embassy in London released these statistics, the Indonesian President had already announced in January and August of that year that all category C prisoners had been released, and the official statistics were intended to confirm that statement. This may be why subsequent figures were never declared, and subsequently there were announcements only about the relatively small number of category B prisoners.

The Foreign Minister mentioned 600,000 prisoners and Admiral Sudomo mentioned 750,000. According to their own reckoning therefore, the Indonesian authorities have failed to account for at least 90,000 prisoners not claimed to have been released, (that is, when arrest totals of 600,000 or 750,000 are compared with a release total of just over 500,000 people).

In line with this conclusion, there are other grounds for questioning the accuracy of official government statements about the number of prisoners. In the previous chapter, the situation of category B and category C prisoners was examined. Study of the former supported the conclusion that, according to the official *Komkamtib* prisoner statistics, the alleged total numbers were at most only half the real totals; accordingly there are strong grounds for believing that the number of prisoners was much more than double the total admitted by *Kopkamtib*. The official *Kopkamtib* figure for category B prisoners was almost 30,000; and taking into account only this category, it can be concluded that there are at present more than 55,000 prisoners in Indonesia.

Furthermore, the preceeding chapter's examination of category C prisoners revealed that this category is completely ignored in official statistics after 1972, but that nonetheless many of these prisoners are still in detention. Then there are those prisoners assigned to category X, described by the authorities as "non-classified". According to the February 1976 official *Kopkamtib* figures, they totalled 3,273; but the actual numbers are virtually impossible to verify independently.

In addition there are the category A prisoners who, according to the February 1976 official *Kopkamtib* statistics, totalled 1,745.

Taking all these factors into consideration, Amnesty International concludes that there are certainly more than 55,000 prisoners held without trial in Indonesia, and the actual number of prisoners held without trial is probably about 100,000.

6

TRIALS

By early 1966, the Army leadership had destroyed left-wing mass organizations, and they next forced the resignation of President Sukarno, who was replaced by General Suharto. The military government of President Suharto's "New Order" then set out formally to discredit the Sukarno administration. One of the ways in which this was done was by means of public show trials, the most prominent being that of Dr Subandrio, who was Deputy Prime Minister and Foreign Minister until 11 March 1966. In October of that year, he was put on trial on charges of subversion. The hearings before a special military tribunal in Jakarta were clearly intended by the military government to be a publicity exercise; a denunciation of the ousted Sukarno administration's policies. Subandrio was sentenced to death on the basis of flimsy evidence relating to his performance of official duties.

During the early months of 1966, a PKI leader, Njono, was brought to trial and accused among other things of having organized the recruitment of members of pro-PKI mass organizations to support the coup at Halim. He denied the charges but was found guilty and sentenced to death. He was executed.

Next came the prominent trial of Sudisman, General Secretary of the Indonesian Communist Party, before a special military tribunal in Jakarta in mid-1967. Sudisman insisted the PKI knew nothing about the attempted coup and that the affair was an internal army matter. The military tribunal sentenced him to death. He was executed in October 1968.

From 1967 until the present, prisoners have been put on trial in different parts of the Republic. By early 1977, of the hundreds of thousands arrested in connection with the 1965 events, the government claimed to have tried about 800 prisoners in all, that is, an annual average of less than 100 cases.

Initially the trials were held before special military tribunals, which invariably imposed the death sentence. Later, the political prisoners were tried by the ordinary courts and the death penalty was frequently imposed. In recent years, a small but increasing number have not been sentenced to death, but to sentences ranging from 15 years to life imprisonment.

The government's handling of the trials has tended to take two forms. A very few were given great prominence and were in every way political show trials. The hearings of special military tribunals were filmed, and broadcast outside the courtrooms through loud-speakers to large crowds. However, most of the trials were held without advance warning and in secrecy. They were occasionally reported briefly in the press, which would state whether the prisoner had been found guilty and sentenced to death or to a very long jail sentence. Throughout a decade of trials Amnesty International has not found a single case of a prisoner not being found guilty.

By any standards, these trials cannot be considered fair. They are rituals used by the government for political and public relations ends. The defendant is invariably convicted. The death penalty or extremely long jail sentences are, as a matter of course, imposed by the courts on people who were innocent of criminal offences.

The courts continue to pass death sentences. Although, judging from the more recent cases known to Amnesty International, a number of death sentences have not been carried out, it is impossible to estimate how many have been implemented since official figures are not available. Possibly more than 50 prisoners currently held are under sentence of death. There have been no reports of commutations of death sentences.

The Trial of Dr Subandrio *

Dr Subandrio was Deputy Prime Minister and Foreign Minister until 11 March 1966. In October of that year, he was put on trial on charges of subversion. The evidence presented at his trial was completely circumstantial. The proceedings were clearly intended by the military authorities to be a publicity exercise, using the courts to indict the policies of the ousted Sukarno administration, Subandrio was, therefore, placed on trial as a proxy for President Sukarno, who still had popular support, which inhibited the military authorities from attacking him directly. The charges of subversion against Subandrio were based on his actions as Deputy Prime Minister and Foreign Minister before and after the 1965 attempted coup. The court proceedings were used to discredit President Sukarno for his domestic reliance on the PKI and for his foreign policy favouring the People's Republic of China.

Subandrio was born in Kepandjen, near Malang in East Java on 15 September 1914. When at secondary school, he became active in nationalist youth movements. In 1942, he graduated from medical

---

* Like many other Indonesians, such as President Suharto, Dr Subandrio is known only by the single name.

school and became an assistant surgeon at the Central General Hospital in Jakarta. During the Japanese occupation he became director of a Semarang hospital.

After the establishment of the Indonesian Republic, he joined the Indonesian Socialist Party (PSI). In 1947 he was sent to the United Kingdom as the Indonesian Republic's first representative there, and established a Republican information office. He set up the first Indonesian Embassy in London in 1949 and was appointed Ambassador in 1950.

In the mid-1950s, he was appointed his country's first Ambassador to Moscow, an appointment which he held for two years. In 1957, he returned to Indonesia to take up the post of Secretary General of the Indonesian Foreign Ministry. At about this time he left the Socialist Party and joined the Indonesian Nationalist Party (PNI). Shortly afterwards, he left the PNI when a regulation was introduced banning government employees from being members of political parties.

After only several months in his new post, he was appointed Foreign Minister, a position which he held until his dismissal and arrest in March 1966. With the establishment of "Guided Democracy" in 1959, Subandrio became increasingly identified with President Sukarno's foreign policy of alignment with Third World countries and with socialist and communist governments. He also became identified with President Sukarno's external initiatives including confrontation with the Dutch which led to the transfer of West Irian from the Netherlands to the Republic, and later military confrontation with the Federation of Malaysia.

From 1963, Subandrio became increasingly involved in economic policy-making. Continuing as Foreign Minister, he became Second, and subsequently First Deputy Prime Minister, and also held a number of key posts in economic affairs. In addition, he was put in charge of the state intelligence unit, BPI. Although identified with Sukarno's policy of working closely with the PKI over domestic and foreign policy, Subandrio has never been regarded as an active supporter of the Communist Party.

When the 1965 coup attempt took place, he was away from Jakarta on a tour of North Sumatra. He returned immediately and, continuing to hold office in Sukarno's Cabinet, supported the President's attempts to stop the widespread killings and to restore national unity. He was sharply criticized by the Army and militant advocates of their New Order and while still Deputy Prime Minister he was kept under surveillance by the Army. He was arrested five months after the abortive coup and his trial began in October 1966.

There were two sets of charges against him. The first was that he had collaborated in a conspiracy to overthrow the legal government. This related to his actions as Deputy Prime Minister and Foreign Minister, and as head of the intelligence bureau, including the policy of purchasing arms from China, and advising the President to halt repayment of debts to the Soviet Union, and to get Indonesia to withdraw from the United Nations. There were numerous other charges, such as allegedly spreading rumours in order to incite left-wing feelings against the Indonesian Army, thereby paving the way for the coup. He was also allegedly forewarned of the planned coup on 1 October 1965 and did not take steps to prevent it but instead went to North Sumatra where he made inflammatory speeches.

The second set of charges related to events after the attempted coup. He was accused of undermining the authority of the state, that is, General Suharto's nascent "New Order", and of supporting the abortive coup and attempting to minimise its significance. He was also accused of actively encouraging counter-demonstrations to those organized in support of General Suharto. The charges were made under the terms of a presidential Decree on Subversion, which was issued by President Sukarno in 1963, making subversion a capital offence. That Subversion Decree did not have the force of law at the time of Subandrio's trial (it became law only in 1969: as discussed in this chapter).

In his defence, Subandrio said that his actions at the time were intended to implement the then President's policies. The court found him guilty on both sets of charges and sentenced him to death.

Many observers, including those sharply critical of President Sukarno's policies have commented that the evidence brought against Subandrio was circumstantial and insufficient to prove subversion, and that he was very much the victim of the "New Order" campaign to discredit President Sukarno.

The case was tried by an extraordinary military tribunal and no judicial process of appeal was allowed against the death sentence. Subandrio appealed for clemency directly to the President. Although there have been occasional reports in the Indonesian and foreign press that President Suharto reached a decision on the plea for clemency, no decision has been publicly announced. Subandrio was a well-known international figure, and it was possibly to avoid international criticism that the death sentence was not carried out.

After sentence, Subandrio was held at a military camp, Cimahi, near Bandung in West Java. He was later transferred to Nirbaya Prison in Jakarta. In August 1973 he appeared as a witness at the trial of Brigadier General Supardjo, a senior police and intelligence officer. Supardjo was sentenced to death and executed.

During Subandrio's ten years' imprisonment, his wife, Hurustiati, who was also a doctor, was not allowed to practice medicine and had to depend on earnings as a teacher of foreign languages. She suffered from a kidney disorder. When their only son died unexpectedly from a heart attack in March 1974, her condition deteriorated and she died a month later. Subandrio himself has been in poor health and was reported to have had a mental breakdown.

Subandrio is a category A prisoner and is one of about 800 who have been tried. His case is typical of the unhappy position of many who were active in political life before 1965, were closely identified with the Sukarno administration and who have been imprisoned during the last ten years. They include cabinet ministers, heads of government departments and agencies, and senior officials, detained because of their pro-Sukarno past, without having been directly involved with the Communist Party. The great majority of these people have never been brought to court.

The defence lawyer in Dr Subandrio's trial, Mr Yap Thiam Hien, a member of the International Commission of Jurists, was himself detained without trial in January 1974, and was released the following December following widespread international concern.

Trial of Asep Suryaman

The trial began in Jakarta in June 1975. Asep Suryaman was accused of being a leading member of the PKI Special Bureau and of conspiring with others to overthrow the government. No evidence was presented that he had taken an active part in the 1965 attempted coup, apart from the fact that he was a Party lecturer in Marxist theory. In 1967, when the PKI membership was being hunted by the military authorities, he sought refuge in East Java and he admitted that he took part in guerrilla activities, which he maintained were in self defence.

The charges were brought under a Presidential Decree made by President Sukarno in 1963. This decree did not have force of law after the fall of President Sukarno, and it only acquired legal status when the legislature passed the text of the decree in 1969, when it became known as the Subversion Act. This Presidential Decree, which received legislative approval six years later, proved a wide-ranging and draconian measure as used by both the Sukarno and Suharto Governments to suppress political oppostion (see Appendix IIIa).

The courts have acted improperly in the trials of all prisoners held in connection with the 1965 events, inasmuch as they convicted them on charges brought under this Presidential decree. Defendants tried before 1969 were still charged under President Sukarno's decree, which up till then did not have the force of law in President Suharto's "New Order". Those who were tried after 1969 were charged with offences relating to activities dating from before 1969, and the retroactive application of the act was unconstitutional. Unquestionably the courts have acted unconstitutionally and illegally in sentencing such prisoners to death or imprisonment.

Asep Suryaman's defence lawyers argued in the trial that since the Subversion Act under which the case had been brought had been passed by the legislature four years after the alleged offences had been said to occur, the court could not act unconstitutionally by applying the law retroactively. The defence lawyers also pointed out that there was no proof of the defendant's personal complicity in the 1965 events. Moreover, the detention of the prisoner since his arrest in September 1971 had been illegal, because no application had been made to a court after the first year of detention without trial, as required by Indonesian law.

One member of the team of defence lawyers went further and challenged the authority of the judges. The distinguished lawyer, Mr Yap Thiam Hien, also pointed out that the panel of judges had been appointed by a government which had issued many decrees affecting members of left-wing organizations which had been legal until 1966. He said that appointed officials of this kind could not judge such cases impartially and according to law. Because of the statement, Mr Yap was cited for contempt of court by the Bar Association.

In his final speech for the defence, Mr Yap described Asep Suryaman as a prisoner whose experience in detention was not unique. He said political prisoners in Indonesia were:

"Treated like the dregs of society, deprived of the most elementary rights enjoyed by all other citizens, like mere objects that can be moved from one place to another, put 'on loan' to other authorities for interrogation, to give evidence or to meet the personal needs of some officials, and they are not even told why they are put 'on loan' or where they are being taken. They have no power and no voice, no right to complain or protest against their interminable imprisonment, against torture, insult, hunger or disease. They have no power and no voice in the face of this abuse against their dignity and person. . . .

"Many of them have become automatons, going to sleep, getting up and taking their meals like persons without any spirit, for they are not permitted to read magazines, newspapers, or books, except religious literature. Nor are they allowed to write to their loved ones. . . such a life leads them to break down under the strain. Some become insane, others have committed suicide, some have tried to rebel against their predicament with horrifying consequences. . .".

Continuing his plea on behalf of the prisoner, Mr Yap pointed to the predicament of prisoners faced with the choice of indefinite detention without trial, or unjustly conducted trials. He reported what a prisoner had told him while he was himself a prisoner:

"We are like leaves on a tree, just waiting to fall to earth and become one with it. Help us to get our freedom back, to rejoin our unprotected families. Help us at the very least to be brought to trial, so that this soul-destroying uncertainty can end. Whatever they want, we are ready to sign, so long as we can be released. . .".

The court convicted Asep Suryaman and sentenced him to death. Despite Amnesty International enquiries to the Indonesian Government, it is not known whether the death sentence was carried out.

Trial of Oei Tju Tat

Mr Oei was a cabinet minister in former President Sukarno's administration. He was a leading member of Partindo (Indonesia Party), a political group which broke away from the Indonesian Nationalist Party in the late 1950s. He was arrested in March 1966 and detained for 10 years before his trial began in Jakarta in February 1976. He was charged under the Subversion Act and was accused of undermining the authority of the government. It was further alleged that he had issued a statement in October 1965 which said that the attempted coup was an internal Army affair. The prosecution claimed that by issuing such a statement, Mr Oei had attempted to destroy or undermine the lawful government of Indonesia.

The defence lawyers, led by Mr Yap Thiam Hien, pointed out that at the time of the alleged offence, President Sukarno's government was in power and that the statement issued by Mr Oei had not been criticized by Sukarno, nor had he been dismissed from the cabinet. Moreover, witnesses at the trial affirmed that Mr Oei was not personally responsible in drafting his party's statement. The defence lawyers criticized the proceedings in the same terms as in Asep Suryaman's trial. The trial was unconstitutional, since Indonesian law did not allow the retroactive application of the Subversion Act. The defence also pointed out that during Mr Oei's 10 years' detention without charge or trial, he had not been served with any warrants of arrest and had been denied access to lawyers. The trial, which began after 10 years of illegal detention, violated the principles of Indonesian justice.

The court, nonetheless, convicted Mr Oei and sentenced him to 13 years' imprisonment, from which 10 years already spent in prison without trial were subtracted.

This judgement has been criticized internationally. The International Commission of Jurists in Geneva, declared:

> "The court's attempted justification of this extraordinary judgement was that Mr Oei 'did not react strongly enough, although protesting against the statement'. This shameful decision can be explained only by factors external to the trial itself, and as an attempt to justify Mr Oei's detention for almost 10 years before trial." (*ICJ Review* No.17, *December 1976*).

The harsh sentence meted out by the court to Mr Oei can be considered relatively light when compared with the kinds of sentences readily imposed by Indonesian judges appointed to hear political trials. The fact that Mr Oei is an internationally known former cabinet minister had some bearing on the court's decision (see Appendix IIIb for Mr Oei's defence speech).

The Trial of Four Women, in February 1975

The defendants were former leading members of organizations affiliated to the PKI. The chief defendant, Sulami, was a leading member of the *Gerakan Wanita Indonesia* (Gerwani), a left-wing womens' organisation, Sri Ambar Rukmiati, was head of the women's bureau of *Sentral Organisasi Buruh Seluruh Indonesia* (SOBSI), the trade union federation. Suharti Harsono was on the staff of *Barisan Tani Indonesia* (BTI), the peasants' union. Sudjinah was on the staff of Gerwani, responsible for education and culture. They were tried under the Subversion Act.

The indictment against the four prisoners alleged participation in the October 1965 attempted coup and also that they had tried to revive the left-wing movement after its various organizations were banned early in 1966. However, the evidence against them presented in court related mainly to their activities after October 1965. They were accused of having published and distributed an illegal bulletin, obtained false identity cards and helped provide assistance for the children of political prisoners. In addition, Sulami was accused of having recruited women to go to Lubang Buaya, to help in cooking and sewing. This, in the Prosecution's view was sufficient proof that she had known about the 1965 attempted coup which was said to have used Lubang Buaya as its base.

The Prosecution requested life imprisonment for Sulami and 20 years for the other defendants. All were found guilty of subversion and of having tried to revive banned organizations. Sulami was sentenced to 20 years' imprisonment. Sudjinah was sentenced to 18 years and the other two to 15 years each.

The 10 years they had spent in prison before trial were deducted from their sentences. It was clear from the evidence presented that the Prosecution had failed to prove that the prisoners were guilty of subversive activity of such a kind as to justify 10 years' imprisonment for involvement in such actions as providing assistance to the children of political prisoners, many of whom were virtually orphans because of the arrest of both parents and other relatives.

GOVERNMENT POLICY ON TRIALS

In 11 years, only several hundred prisoners, (a very small proportion) have been brought to trial. The trials were held merely to suit the government's purposes. It was a foregone conclusion that the prisoners concerned would be found guilty and either sentenced to death or condemned to long periods of further imprisonment.

The Indonesian Government has repeatedly indicated its good intentions by mentioning its willingness to increase the rate at which trials were being held. But after 11 years, despite such protestations, the rate at which trials are being held has not significantly accelerated. Moreover, the trial proceedings display a gross miscarriage of justice. Defendants in political trials are merely victims of the government's attempts to show that the rule of law is observed and to justify the continued detention without trial of the vast majority of the prisoners.

Furthermore, despite Government assurances that foreign jurists would be permitted to observe political trials, such assurances amounted to very little. The former Australian Prime Minister, Mr Gough Whitlam, was assured by President Suharto in a meeting in 1975 that Australian jurists would be permitted to observe political trials in Indonesia. In August 1975, the validity of this assurance was tested by the Australian Section of the International Commission of Jurists, when it applied to the Indonesian Government for two of its leading members, Mr John Dowd and Mr Paul Stein, MP, to observe the trial of Asep Suryaman. They were both refused visas to observe the trial.

During Asep Suryaman's trial, his lawyer Mr Yap Thiam Hien, rightly critized the Subversion Act. He described it as a "rubber law", pointing out that it was so vague and broad in its application that virtually any kind of political or social activity could be indictable under it.

It is the view of Amnesty International that the Subversion Act should be repealed, and that political prisoners in Indonesia should be given prompt, open and fair trials; or be released immediately.

Purwadi and his family. Purwadi was arrested in 1965. His family joined him on Buru in 1972.

Basuki Effendi, well-known Indonesian film director, arrested in 1969 and now detained on Buru.

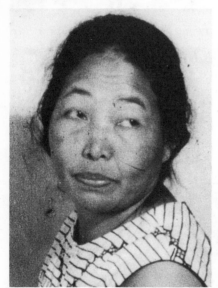

Dr Sumiarsih Caropeboka, arrested in 1967. She was a prison doctor at Plantungan and is now detained in Bulu prison, Semarang.

Pramoedya Ananta Toer, one of Indonesia's foremost writers, detained without trial since 1965. He is now on Buru Island.

Forced Labour in Prison Camps: above, at Plantungan; below, on Buru

Left to right: Suharti Harsono, Sri Ambar Rukmiati, Sudjinah and Sulami, arrested in 1966 and 1967; tried in 1975

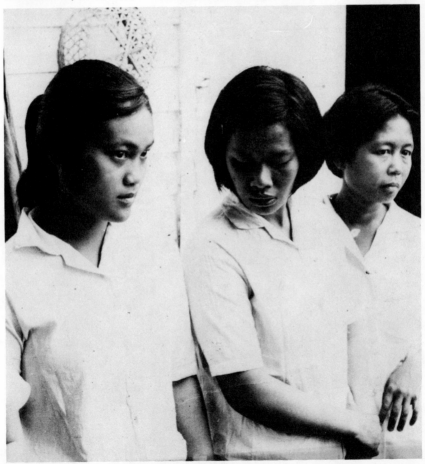

Three young women arrested and detained on Kalimantan

Prisoners in a camp on Kalimantan

7

INDIVIDUAL CASE HISTORIES

Over the years, Amnesty International has taken up a wide range of cases of political prisoners held in Indonesia without trial. They have included well-known ministers, children, people in their 50s or 60s, women, famous writers, painters and musicians, former Army officers and other soldiers, peasants and trade unionists, and Indonesians from practically every walk of life or social class. The following are a sample of cases from the Amnesty International files.

Pramoedya Ananta Toer

Pramoedya Ananta Toer is a novelist, essayist and critic, regarded by many as the finest Indonesian writer of his generation. Selections of his work are still prescribed reading in Indonesian schools. He has been a political prisoner since October 1965 and is now one of about 14,000 prisoners living in penal exile on Buru, one of the more remote islands of the Indonesian archipelago. He was detained on the orders of the military, he has not been charged or tried and is scheduled for permanent imprisonment. In the 11 years following his arrest, he has been denied pencil and paper with which to write.

This last decade has been Pramoedya's third period of imprisonment; each imprisonment has been under a different administration. During the 1945 Revolution, while he was active in the Indonesian nationalist movement, Pradoedya was arrested by the Dutch colonial government and imprisoned in Jakarta. While in detention, he began work on his first novels. His second arrest was in 1960 when he was detained by the Sukarno Government for several months without trial. He had just published a popular history, *The Chinese Question in Indonesia,* which aroused official military and civilian antagonism on account of its defence of the Chinese community at a time when discriminatory policies were being pursued by the government. The book was banned and Pramoedya arrested.

In 1965, Pramoedya was again arrested, this time by the Army under the authority of General Suharto, now President Suharto. No reasons have been given for Pramoedya's imprisonment apart from the general charge that he, with other detainees, was a committed Marxist. As a radical and a populist, Pramoedya's natural affinity was to the political left, but it seems unlikely that he was ever a member of the Communist Party. Certainly the government has never attempted to claim or prove that he was a member of the PKI. A combination of factors probably led to his detention: his concern for the Chinese community in 1960, which earned him the lasting hostility of influential elements in the Army; his membership of *LEKRA,* a left-wing cultural organization proscribed in 1966 as a communist "front"; and the criticism, never muted, which, in his writing, he levelled at corruption and other social evils.

Pramoedya was born in Blora in Java on 6 February 1925. He worked for a time as a journalist, and then joined the nationalist movement when the Dutch returned to Indonesia in 1945 following the Japanese surrender. After his release from prison in 1950, he published his first novels, written in prison, and by 1953 his reputation was already such that he was invited to Holland as a member of an official cultural delegation. Pramoedya's reputation as a writer was based on his novels and short stories written during the years immediately after Independence, which drew on events during the Revolution and on his personal involvement with the nationalist movement. He has written ten novels, some critical essays and a biography of Kartini, the 19th century Javanese heroine who argued the case for women's emancipation, also his book on the Chinese community.

In 1965 he was at work on an encyclopaedia. When he was arrested by soldiers, his wife and eight children were thrown out of his house, and a mob was allowed to ransack his books and manuscripts destroying everything, including the collected material for the encyclopaedia.

From 1965 to 1969, Pramoedya was imprisoned in Jakarta. In 1969, he was among the first group of detainees to be transferred to the penal settlement on Buru Island, where he is forced, like the other 14,000 prisoners held on the island, to work as an unpaid agricultural labourer (see Chapter 9).

Pramoedya's wife lives in Jakarta. Of his children, the youngest, now 11, was a baby of two months at the time of his father's arrest. They live with a relative in impoverished conditions; they have not been allowed back to their house since Pramoedya's arrest. Mrs Pramoedya is gravely ill with tuberculosis.

Three of Pramoedya's brothers are also political prisoners, one is with him on Buru. The wives of two of his brothers have divorced their husbands (see Chapter 10). Although monthly letters are officially permitted, in practice the only communication between Pramoedya and his wife in Jakarta is restricted to officially permitted postcards which reach her irregularly. During the first three years that he was on Buru, she received only two postcards from him.

As previously mentioned a small group of journalists was permitted to visit Buru Island in 1971. They confirmed two essential facts: that Buru was a penal settlement to which 10,000 untried prisoners had been exiled, and that many prisoners had only the most tenuous or casual association with the communist movement (for example, the youngest prisoner on the island had been arrested when he was 12). While there, the journalists met Pramoedya and confirmed that he was unable to write because he was deprived of pen and paper. Asked about his hopes for the future, he described his predicament in these words:

"On Buru I have no future. Conditions for me here are too difficult. I want to return to Java, my home. . . I used to be free in everything, thinking and talking and doing, but now I am a prisoner. I have lost my freedom, I have lost my family, I have lost my work. I am a writer. That is all. I want to write and one day I will write. That is my work and my vocation."

This year, Pramoedya Ananta Toer spent his 51st birthday on Buru.

Charlotte Salawati

Charlotte Salawati, who is better known in Indonesia as Ibu (mother) Salawati, was born on 20 March 1909. She is now over 68, and had been detained without trial for ten years. A long-standing Amnesty International adoption case, she was released in March 1976.

In her youth, Ibu Salawati was prominent in the nationalist movement which won Indonesia's independence from Dutch colonial rule in 1950. She was active in the politics of the Republic as a member of the PKI, representing the party in Parliament, and as Deputy Chairwoman of the women's association *Gerwani*. Throughout her public life until her arrest in 1965 she was widely known and respected in Indonesia, even by those who did not share her political views.

She was born in Sulawesi (the Celebes), the Eastern region of the Republic, an island nearly 1,000 miles to the north-east of Java. She was brought up a Christian and educated at Dutch schools, but felt as a young woman nationalist that Church life as it was practised in Makasar (the regional capital of the Celebes) in the 1920s did not deal adequately with social and political problems in colonial Indonesia. For a period she left the church, apparently with reluctance. She became active in the nationalist movement, gradually moving to work in left-wing organizations. After 1950 she joined the PKI, which seemed to her to offer a systematic program of economic and political development. Although a staunch and active member of the PKI, she has always retained her Christian beliefs. She is a woman of modest personal ambition and strong committment to socialist ideals.

She first trained as a teacher and taught in a Dutch-run school, but was dismissed after she had written newspaper articles which were disliked by the Dutch administration. She then taught in a school in Makasar run by the nationalist movement, but in 1932 again came under suspicion, and this time was barred from teaching.

Ibu Salawati then trained and worked as a midwife. At the same time she produced a journal for women, *Wanita,* in Makasar. The Dutch colonial police regarded her as politically suspect, kept her house under surveillance and restricted her visitors. In 1945, following the end of the Japanese occupation, she taught again in a nationalist school which was closed by the Dutch administration two years later. By now she had become an elected member of the South Celebes Representative Assembly. At this time, Indonesian nationalist forces under the future President Sukarno and Dr Muhammad Hatta were fighting the Dutch, who were trying to restore the colonial administration. Mrs Salawati worked for political union between the Dutch-sponsored State of East Indonesia (as South Celebes was then called) and the new Republic of Indonesia.

After Independence in 1950, she was delegated by the new government to negotiate with dissident Islamic groups in the Celebes who wanted regional autonomy. During the 1950s, she remained in public and political life. She was deputy mayor of Makasar, head of *Gerwani* in South Celebes, chairwoman of the Indonesian Peace Committee and, in the 1955 elections, she was elected as a PKI supporter to Parliament. From 1962 she was deputy national chairwoman of *Gerwani* and sat in Parliament as a PKI representative. In 1965 she was a member of the official Indonesian delegation to the Peace Congress in Helsinki.

The fact that Ibu Salawati was a member of the PKI and a leader of *Gerwani* (even though both were legal organizations taking part in parliamentary politics before October 1965) were the grounds for the authorities to detain her as a category B prisoner. There was no evidence against her, and the authorities never intended to bring her to trial. In this way, Ibu Salawati, one of the outstanding women leaders of Indonesia's struggle for independence, has from the age of 56 to 67, spent her time in Bukit Duri women's prison in Jakarta. She was given no explanation when she was released in March 1976.

Subadi

Subadi is a peasant who, with the help of his wife and children, farmed a small plot in a village in Kutoardjo, a district of Central Java. He belonged to the PKI and was arrested shortly after the 1965 abortive coup. Like the great majority of the tens of thousands of political prisoners in Indonesia, he was not at all prominent in public life.

Subadi had no formal education, but taught himself to read. He disapproved of the local council's policies and critizized them vigorously. PKI policies possibly matched his own ideas on how local problems of poverty could be tackled, but no details are available about his political life before his arrest.

Initially, he was imprisoned in Kutoardjo for about a year. During this time his wife was able to visit and to take food to him. He was then moved to a prison in Purworedjo for several months. While there he was severely beaten during interrogation. Later he was sent back to Kutoardjo where he was allowed out during the day, returning to prison at night. This lasted for about a year. Then in 1970, he was sent to the penal island of Nusakembangan, off the south coast of Central Java. He is still there. Since 1970, his family has not been able to visit him because of the distance and expense involved. The totally arbitrary way in which Subadi has been treated is the common experience of most prisoners. At times conditions could be said to improve slightly, even to the extent of a prisoner being allowed to go home during the day, but this is merely through some administrative decision—the prisoner may next be transferred to a place too far away for family visits to be possible.

Communication between Subadi and his family is limited to one censored postcard per month on which he is allowed to write 20 words. In these postcards, he continually asks for clothes, sandals, food and medicines. His family get these together and send them, but although they regularly receive postcards requesting such items they have never received confirmation that their parcels have reached him. Again, this is the common experience of prisoners. They are prey to the cupidity of the prison guards and the postal authorities.

When Subadi was taken, five other people in the village were arrested. One has since died and two have paid bribes to military officers to obtain their release from prison. When a similar offer was made to Subadi's family, which would have cost them 50,000 rupiahs, they consulted Subadi but he refused, saying that he would never feel secure outside if released under such circumstances. The corrupt practice of military officers who demand money for release of prisoners is quite usual.

Subadi's wife and five children are extremely poor and had to sell their land in order to survive. The elder children cannot find employment. The daughters of marriageable age have not been able to marry because of the stigma of their father's political imprisonment. This family's plight is familiar to many who are in a similar situation in the small towns and villages throughout Indonesia.

Sugiyah

Sugiyah was 13 when she was detained in early October 1965. She has spent her adolescence and her youth as a captive political prisoner held without trial. Amnesty International learnt in 1976, that she was released, but the precise date of her release is not known.

She was born in 1952 in Jakarta. Her parents were poor, and her education limited to elementary school. She was not involved in any political activity before September 1965, but when in the second half of 1965 a group of her friends were recruited into the campaign of confrontation with Malaysia, she accompanied them. At the time, volunteers were being trained throughout the Republic by many political parties and their supporting mass organizations.

Pemuda Rakyat, the PKI youth organization, was the strongest youth organization in Sugiyah's home locality, and it recruited the training group that Sugiyah joined. It went to a training ground in Lubang Buaya, near the Halim Air Force base, which, later, became the headquarters of the coup leaders in 1965. This was where the kidnapped generals were taken, and where they were killed and their bodies concealed. Anyone at the training ground on that particular night was regarded, by implication, by the military authorities as having been "directly involved" in the coup. Sugiyah was there and the charges against here were, therefore, considered to be serious.

After the failure of the coup, a nationwide campaign was launched in the press, highlighting atrocities alleged to have been committed at Lubang Buaya, including allegations of sexual orgies on the night of the coup, and infliction of atrocities on the victims of the coup. There is no evidence in support of the allegations (see Chapter 10).

In mid-1971 many of the Lubang Buaya prisoners, including Sugiyah, were transferred to the Plantungan Women's Detention Camp, in Central Java.

Sugiyah's case illustrates the way in which people were imprisoned as justification of the official interpretation of the Lubang Buaya events. The military authorities, under President Suharto's "New Order", claimed that the young girls at Lubang Buaya committed atrocities, and these were widely publicized in order to establish that the PKI had an evil influence, especially on young people. In the opinion of many independent commentators, the alleged Lubang Buaya incident was used by the military to augment public hostility towards left-wing suspects, and thus created the mood which prompted widespread reprisals and killings.

It should be noted, that if the government's account of the Lubang Buaya incident is true, nonetheless the government has never attempted to prove this by putting the Lubang Buaya girl prisoners on trial. In 11 years, an estimated 800 prisoners have been brought to court—but not a single girl who was at Lubang Buaya. The reluctance of the government to establish the truth of the Lubang Buaya allegations in the courts, has been Amnesty International's main reason for deciding to take up the cases of girl prisoners such as Sugiyah.

Karel Supit

Karel Supit was born in Menado, North Sulawesi, in 1917. As a young man he worked in the oil fields at Cepu in East Java. After the proclamation of the Republic in 1945, he formed and led a nationalist guerrilla group in East Java against the Dutch colonial government.

In 1950, he returned to Menado, where he took the initiative in establishing the left-wing trades union federation SOBSI, in Minahasa, and helped to build the Communist Party in the region. In 1954, he became a member of the Party's Central Committee. He was elected to Parliament as a Communist Party member in 1955 and was prominent in the politics of his region.

He strongly opposed the Permesta rebellion against the central government which broke out in North Sulawesi in 1957 and he was captured by the rebels. He was released several months later when the rebellion was suppressed by central government troops. Later he moved to Jakarta to work at the Communist Party head office, where he was put in charge of the Party's International Department.

In 1963, he was appointed to be a member of the Indonesian delegation to the United Nations Assembly. He was also a member of Indonesian delegations to a number of international conferences and gatherings.

Following the October 1965 abortive coup, PKI leaders and members tried to evade arrest, but Karel Supit was caught within days. After being held at the Salemba Men's Prison in Jakarta for five years, he was transported to Buru in 1969. His wife, Lies Supit, had gone into hiding in 1965 knowing she faced arrest because of her work for *Gerwani;* their children were cared for by relatives. Early in 1967, Mrs Supit was also arrested and is now detained at the Bukit Duri Women's Prison, also in Jakarta. Despite the proximity of Karel's wife while he was still detained in Jakarta, they were not permitted to meet. Later, one of their sons was also arrested.

When Karel Supit was transferred to Buru he was 52, well over the maximum age of 45, fixed by the government for those to be transported to the island. Now 60 years' old, his health is seriously threatened by the harsh conditions he and other political prisoners on Buru must endure.

Siti Suratih

Siti Suratih was born in Central Java. She was a trained nurse and carried on her job after her marriage to B.O. Hutapea, a leading communist from North Sumatra, who became a member of the Party's new Politbureau established under Aidit in 1951.

Siti Suratih herself was never attracted by politics and did not join any mass organization. She had four children and continued to work as a nurse, moving to Jakarta together with her husband, where she obtained work at the central army hospital. She became the chief-nurse of the maternity ward.

After the abortive coup in October 1965, she was dishonourably dismissed. Clearly her dismissal was due to her marriage to a leading communist. This was a common occurrence in the years immediately following 1965, when the wives of Party members were liable to be arrested.

For a year or so after the coup, she lived in very difficult circumstances. She had no contact with her husband, who had gone underground, and she had to care for her children single-handed. She was continually harassed because of her husband's position in the PKI. The military kept a close watch on her to discover whether she would be contacted by her husband.

She was arrested in 1966 while her husband was still in hiding. She was interrogated exclusively about her relations with him. None of her relatives were able to look after the three children still with her, so she had to take them with her to the detention camp, where they stayed for several months. When she was transferred to Bukit Duri Women's Prison in Jakarta, she was not allowed to have her children there and had to leave them behind at the detention camp in the care of other prisoners to await the expected visit of relatives who, it was hoped, would take the children home. The children later stayed with their aunt and went to school in Jakarta.

In 1968, her husband was killed in Blitar in East Java. She has still not been officially notified of his death. For the major part of her detention, she was believed to be a category C prisoner and was expecting early release. However, in mid-1971 she was transferred to Plantungan Women's Prison in Central Java and so deduced that she had been classified as a category B prisoner. Her transfer may also have been because they wanted her to work as a nurse.

Siti Suratih is now 55. Since the transfer to another prison, of two prisoners who are doctors, she has been the only trained medical person in Plantungan Camp.

Sitor Situmorang

The well-known writer and poet Sitor Situmorang was arrested in 1967, and was adopted by Amnesty International in early 1970. After eight years of imprisonment without trial, Sitor Situmorang was released from prison in January 1975 and was placed under house arrest. His case is cited as an example of a political prisoner who should never have been detained without trial and who was imprisoned for eight years.

After working as a journalist, Sitor Situmorang became an established and prolific writer. In 1959, he became founding chairman of the National Cultural Institute, the cultural organization of the Indonesian National Party (PNI).

He was head of the Indonesian delegation to the Asian-African Writers' Conference in Cairo in 1963, and visited China after the Conference. Following this visit he published a volume of social-realist verse entitled *New Era*. He also published two collections of talks on socialist orientated literature. By this time, his ideas had shifted considerably from his former defence of art for art's sake. He also became a Member of Parliament, and spokesman for artists.

After the 1965 attempted coup, he had retained his links with the PNI although a widespread purge was being carried out against radicals in the Party and in its mass organizations. But neither his Institute nor his works were actually banned, as had happened with *LEKRA* and its members.

He was arrested in 1967, when the authorities claimed to have discovered in his possession writings "critical of the New Order". He was detained at Salemba Prison in Jakarta until January 1975, when he was released at the age of 54 and put under house arrest. This was later modified to a requirement that he frequently report to a supervising office.

An Amnesty International mission was in Jakarta shortly after Sitor Situmorang was released, and was told by a leading Indonesian churchman, who is a friend of Sitor Situmorang:

"Of course it is right that Sitor should have been released. He is one of us. He was not in any way involved in the attempted coup of 1965."

The case of Sitor Situmorang was described in detail in *Indonesia Special* (1973) an Amnesty International Publication.

Up till his release, he was held in a prison designated for category B prisoners, but in an interview following his release, he was asked:

"In detention, is there a difference in the treatment which category A, B and C prisoners receive and that which category X prisoners receive?"

Sitor replied:

"There is no difference. Furthermore we ourselves did not know in what category we were classified. Only after my release from Salemba Prison did I know that I was a category X prisoner. But officially in my letter of release it says that I am *'non golongan'* (of no category or group)."

Following his release after eight years' detention he was put under house arrest for eight months, then under "town arrest" for one year. House arrest and subsequent restriction of movement is standard government practice with regard to all "released" prisoners.

I. Made Sutayasa

Sutayasa is an archeologist. He was arrested on 2 March 1975 at Jakarta Airport when he returned from an archeologists' conference held in Sydney, Australia. Following his arrest, he was formally dismissed from his post in the National Research Center of Archeology in mid-1975.

Sutayasa is one of those who remain indefinitely in the category of persons liable to arrest for alleged involvement in the 1965 events. When the abortive coup occurred in 1965, Sutayasa was then a student at a university in Bali, where he was a member of a student movement, *Consentrasi Gerakan Mahasiswa Indonesi,* which was associated with the PKI. The former was banned after 1965, and many of its members were arrested. Apart from his membership in this organization, there do not seem to have been any grounds for his arrest, ten years after 1965.

Following his arrest in Jakarta, Sutayasa was transferred in October 1975 to a prison in Den Pasar, the provincial capital of Bali. This prison is just off the road, along Jalan Diponegoro.

Sutayasa has not been charged or tried. He is aged 36, and has a wife and four children.

Dr Djajus

Dr Djajus, who is 63 years of age, has been detained for more than eleven years without trial. He was trained as a doctor of medicine and became well-known for his research on asthma. Djajus was a member of the Association of Indonesian Graduates (HSI).

Before his arrest shortly after the abortive coup in 1965, Dr Djajus had a medical practice in Ambarawa, Central Java. He was at first detained in Mlaten prison in Semarang and then moved to Nusakembangan camp where he spent six years in detention. Later, in December 1975, he was taken to Jakarta, where he was tortured until he "confessed" to the allegations made against him. Then, in October 1976, he was transferred back to Mlaten. Dr Djajus has spent most of his eleven years in solitary confinement, without contact with his wife and eight children. As a result of his prolonged detention, his health has been seriously impaired.

Suprapto Mangkuseputro and Surjadi Wibisono

Before his arrest in October 1965, Mr Mangkuseputro was a director of an industrial trading company, NV Abasan. Several members of his family were arrested with him, but they were released after a few months in detention. Mr Mangkuseputro was transferred from one detention center to another during the early years of his imprisonment. Finally, he was moved to a Nusakembangan prison camp.

In early 1975, almost ten years after the coup, Mr Mangkuseputro's son, Surjadi Wibisono, was arrested. He was accused of involvement in the left-wing movement before the 1965 events. Shortly after his arrest, he was transferred to Buru. He was among the first prisoners to be sent to Buru since the initial transportations had taken place between 1969 and 1971.

Supardi

Supardi is one of several prisoners in Salemba Prison, Jakarta, who have been detained for many years in an isolation unit, Block N, inside the prison. Before the 1965 events, Supardi was a member of the Railwaymen's Union (SBKA). His association with that trade union, proscribed shortly after the abortive coup, was sufficient to expose him to arrest as a communist suspect. Arrested in 1966, he has been detained without trial ever since.

Gultom

Gultom is a young painter who comes from Sumatra. Before his arrest he was studying at the Art Academy, ASRI, in Jogjakarta, Central Java. He was a member of the left-wing cultural association, LEKRA. Gultom's parents were unable to pay for his schooling and LEKRA supported him financially while he studied at the Art Academy.

Gultom is one of many artists detained on Buru. He is probably now in his late twenties.

Roespanadi Soedjono

Soedjono worked for many years as a technical director in various ports in Indonesia. Between 1961 and 1962 he worked in Tandjung Priok and between 1962 and 1963 in Ujung Pandang in Sulawesi. In 1964 he travelled overseas to conferences in Sweden and Paris and in 1965 he was appointed President Director of the harbour at Surabaya, East Java. Soedjono was arrested in 1966 and was accused of not intervening on behalf of the authorities in the first few days after the attempted coup. He was categorized as a category C prisoner. In 1969 he was released but was re-arrested in 1970 and sent to Buru Island. He has been there ever since.

Soedjono is now 44 years old. Since his exile to Buru, his wife has had to earn small amounts by selling food. She has no contact with her husband.

8

PRISONS: CONDITIONS AND FORCED LABOUR

The Indonesian Government has claimed repeatedly that its treatment of political prisoners is humane and that the conditions in political prisons are reasonably satisfactory. In reality, the conditions in most Indonesian political prisons are deplorable, and in many places the prisoners are subjected to forced labour. It would appear that the Indonesian Government is aware of and sensitive to the true state of prison conditions. The Government has created misleading publicity in recent years, and at the same time prevented proper independent evaluation of the conditions in political prisons. Since 1972, the Indonesian Government has not allowed Indonesian and foreign journalists to visit prisons, apart from several conducted tours of Buru by Indonesian journalists, and one brief visit to the island by a Dutch journalist in 1976.

The reluctance of the Indonesian Government to reveal to visiting missions and journalists the true state of political prisons, is demonstrated by its hindrance of the work of the International Committee of the Red Cross.

In January—February 1977, the International Committee of the Red Cross sent a team to visit Indonesian prisons. From its sources in Jakarta, Amnesty International learnt of the steps taken by the Indonesian Government to obstruct the work of the visiting Red Cross team.

Firstly, the team was able only to visit less than 10 prisons, out of the several hundred places of detention in Indonesia, and all the prisons visited were selected by the Indonesian authorities themselves. Clearly, the Indonesian Government had obstructed the normal procedures pertaining to prison visits by Red Cross teams. For example, one of the prisons visited by the Red Cross team was Salemba Prison in Jakarta. Immediately before the visit, 26 Salemba prisoners were transferred to the military prison in Jakarta (*Rumah Tahanan Militer*), in Jalan Budi Utomo. Among the prisoners transferred were: Taher Thajeb, Yubaar Ayub, Karim D.P., Suwondo Budiardjo, Dr Prawoto Wongsowijoto and Gunulyo S.H. These prisoners had a number of things in common: they were articulate, of professional and cosmopolitan background, and therefore capable of explaining their circumstances in European languages.

A transfer of this kind which is not for the purposes of transit from Salemba to the military prison is unprecedented, and there is no doubt whatsoever that the prisoners were transferred in order to prevent the Red Cross team from interviewing them, thereby obtaining an accurate picture of conditions in Salemba Prison.

After the Red Cross team's visit, all 26 prisoners were transferred from the military prison back to Salemba. The remaining prisoners were told by the prison authorities to speak well of the Salemba Prison conditions when talking to the Red Cross delegates, and they were threatened with reprisals if they did not.

Moreover, information received by Amnesty International from Jakarta indicated that the Indonesian Government had planned to allow the Red Cross team to visit Buru Island, but only for one day. The terms under which the Indonesian Government were prepared to allow the team to visit Buru were unacceptable to the Red Cross so they declined the offer.

Elsewhere too, Amnesty International's Indonesian sources have so far been able to provide information of several prisons where prisoners were threatened by the authorities in attempts to inhibit them from speaking openly to the delegates, and, in at least one other prison, at Sukamulia, several hundred prisoners were transferred to prevent them from being interviewed by the Red Cross team.

Whereas the above-mentioned information was sent to Amnesty International by its own sources in Indonesia, it should be pointed out that the International Red Cross mission was aware of what it described as "the difficulties encountered during the visits". Reporting on its 1977 visit to Indonesia, the International Committee of the Red Cross issued a terse and unusually critical statement:

"An ICRC mission consisting of four delegates, two of them doctors, was in Indonesia from 25 January to 18 February to visit seven places of detention selected by the Indonesian authorities. The centres visited were Salemba, Nirbaya, Ambarrawa, Plantungan, Koblen, Sukamulia and Tandikat.

"In accordance with custom, the ICRC communicated the observations of its delegates only to the Indonesian Government. In submitting its report, the ICRC drew the attention of the authorities to the fact that its delegates' findings could not be regarded as an indication of the real conditions of detention in Indonesia for two reasons: the limited number of places visited and the difficulties encountered during the visits.

"The ICRC will continue its visits to places of detention in Indonesia on the condition that these difficulties are overcome".
(*International Review of the Red Cross*, No.193, April 1977).

The steps taken by the Indonesian Government to prevent prisoners revealing the truth about their conditions, is illustrated also by what happened at Malang Prison in East Java, when it was visited by a team from the International Committee of the Red Cross in 1974. Subsequently, ʼmnesty International received from an Indonesian source the following message:

"Another important event to report is the visit by the International Red Cross delegation to investigate the conditions of political prisoners in Malang. Before the delegation's arrival, 18 prisoners, five of whom were sick, were removed and taken to the Den Pom (military police headquarters) so as to prevent them talking to the delegation. The removal of these 18 prisoners proves that the prison authorities were afraid that the secrets of their brutality would be exposed and described to the delegation. Tight precautions were taken by the prison authorities at the time of the delegation's visit, which occurred on 5 September 1974, in order to prevent the delegation from making direct contact with the prisoners. The head of the delegation, Dr Remy Russbach, took a firm stand and said that the visit had the approval of the Indonesian Government. He expressed dissatisfaction with the way he was being treated as he was not permitted to conduct an unrestricted inspection. After permission was finally granted, he managed to escape supervision and entered some blocks to converse with several political prisoners. When he left, he managed to take with him a plastic bag containing a ration of food to prove how badly the prisoners were being treated. Without help from their families, it is impossible for the prisoners to survive. Many would die of starvation, as indeed has happened in Surabaya. The prison commandant's informants told him about these secret interviews, and as a result three prisoners were severely beaten in the prison yard. Thanks to their courage, nothing escaped from their lips.

"After the delegation's visit to Malang, prisoners began to receive vitamins and those who were ill were taken for treatment to Sukun army hospital. During the term of duty of Deputy Commandant Sulaiman, 16 political prisoners have died as a result of lack of medical treatment. Unfortunately, the delegation did not visit another smaller prison where eight women political prisoners are being held in conditions that are far worse than those of the men."

Despite the prison authorities' attempts selectively to transfer prisoners, and despite their threats and reprisals, the Indonesian Government does not appear to have succeeded in vitiating the effectiveness of visits from International Red Cross teams. Government spokesmen frequently claim that the reports of visiting Red Cross teams show that conditions are good in Indonesian prisons, but the Government has never taken up the request of Amnesty International and others to publish the reports submitted by the International Committee of the Red Cross to the Government about the prisons visited in 1974. The Indonesian Governement is empowered to publish these reports if it wishes to prove that conditions in Indonesian prisons are satisfactory, as they claimed.

The most recent example of the Government trying to conceal the truth about political prisoners' conditions, was a speech given by General Ali Said, the Indonesian Prosecutor General, at a luncheon of the Jakarta Lions Club, on 5 January 1977. On 6 January, the Jakarta newspaper, *Sinar Harapan,* reported:

"Ali Said then invited people to compare reports from Amnesty International with that made by the International Red Cross which had given its own evaluation of the prisoners on the island of Buru."

The newspaper also reported that:

"In [the Prosecutor General's] estimation, the propaganda spread by Amnesty International was lacking in objectivity. As an example, he mentioned that with regard to the 1965 prisoners, that they were disseminating photographs which had been made in 1969. Clearly the things they were spreading were out of date photographs."

It was for all these reasons, according to the Prosecutor General, that:

"There cannot be any meeting point between the outlook of the Indonesian Government and Amnesty International. 'For this reason' he said, on the occasion of this function, 'we shall not deal with them. . . . Nevertheless', he said, 'the Indonesian Government is willing to deal with foreign ambassadors who present memorandums or appeals from Amnesty International, but it is quite out of the question for us to deal directly with Amnesty International', he said."

Political prisoners in Indonesia can find themselves confined for indefinite periods in any one of a wide variety of institutions. They may be held in a prison intended exclusively for untried political prisoners; in a prison for criminal as well as political prisoners; in a labour camp or penal settlement; in guarded quarters attached to factories, plantation or public works units; in an interrogation center or a house unofficially used for interrogation; in a military camp providing servants and labourers for army officers.

The Indonesian Government ignores its constitutional and legal obligations to those of its citizens who are deprived of their liberty and who are held arbitrarily by local military commanders. This means such prisoners have no idea how long they may be held at interrogation centers (possibly for years), and they can be transferred from one kind of penal institution to another over the years.

The case of Subadi, described in the last chapter, illustrates some aspects of the arbitrariness of imprisonment. Initially, Subadi was taken to a prison where his wife could visit him and take him food. Then he was moved to a prison in another town where he was severely beaten during interrogation. Subsequently he was transferred back to the first prison, where he was allowed to return home during the day, returning to the prison at night. After a year, he was transferred to a penal settlement on Nusakembangen, where he and the other prisoners are subjected to forced labour. The penal settlement is so inaccessible that his family cannot visit him.

Thus, in one prison the inmates can be treated more or less in the prescribed manner, in another they can be permitted certain privileges, but later their conditions can change significantly, either in the same prison or after transfer to another prison or to a penal settlement. At any stage, prisoners can be forced to work and can be exploited to the financial advantage of the military officers in charge of them.

As regard both prison conditions and release, the prisoners are totally and arbitrarily controlled by local military commanders, who are allowed wide discretionary powers by the central Government.

The following are the different kinds of penal institutions which currently affect political prisoners.

INTERROGATION CENTERS

When Indonesian citizens are arrested for political reasons, they are taken by the military arrest team to a place for questioning. These are buildings whose function is not clearly evident from their external appearance; they look like private dwellings or shops. They are not officially designated nor do most people know of their existence. Some are regularly and exclusively used as interrogation centers, for instance, as in Jalan Tanah Abang and Jalan Gunung Sahari in Jakarta. Moreover, civilian prisoners can be taken to military camps for interrogation, and this is usual with military prisoners. In every town which serves as an administrative center in Indonesia, either at provincial or local levels, there is at least one interrogation center.

In the years following 1965, torture was systematically used as an everyday practice during interrogation. Young girls below the age of 13, old men, people who were frail and ill, were not exempt from torture. It was used not only for interrogation, but also as punishment and with sadistic intent. Cases of sexual assault on women and extreme cruelty were reported to Amnesty International. Deaths from torture were frequently reported up till the end of the 1960s. At the present time, Amnesty International receives reports of cases of torture under interrogation. The worst cases are those of military officers and men suspected of left-wing tendencies, who are tortured by their fellow officers. The Air Force interrogation center in Jakarta is particularly notorious for its use of brutal and prolonged torture.

PRISONS

The massive arrest of large numbers of prisoners detained after 1965 led to many *ad hoc* installations being created or adapted to hold the prisoners. Existing prisons for ordinary criminal prisoners became extremely crowded with political prisoners. Camps used during the war by the Japanese occupation forces to hold prisoners of war and internees were also used, and several, such as the one at Cimahi near Bandung, are still in use.

Until 1972, a few foreign journalists were allowed to visit political prisons, but in the last three years such visits have been forbidden, except for the visit of one journalist to Buru.

All prisons containing political detainees are run by military officers and guards, who are usually members of the military police corps. The prisoners' welfare is left almost entirely to the discretion of local military commanders. Whatever central, regional or provincial policy may be, the officers in charge of prisoners are, in practice, permitted to regulate things very much as they like. For example, they can decide what proportion of any official allocation of funds allowed for prisoners is actually spent on them. The current allowance for food for each prisoner is supposed to be 65 rupiahs (US $0.17) a day. This is quite insufficient, and even the full allocation of 65 rupiahs is often not given to prisoners, but is in part corruptly appropriated by the prison administration. The prison commanders can make what rules they like about the frequency and duration of prison visits. Brutal treatment of prisoners is commonplace in those prisons where the commandants are notorious for their cruelty, as is the case at Kalisosok and at Ambarawa.

There are different types of prisons. Two prisons are used to detain internationally-known civilian prisoners and senior Army officers. One is Nirbaya prison in Jakarta, with about 60 prisoners, where former ministers and senior officials are detained together with some former senior military officers. The other is the *Rumah Tahanan Militer* (RTM) in Jakarta, with 150 prisoners, which was previously a military prison and now also contains civilian political detainees and others who are in transit between camps and are kept there temporarily. In both of these prisons, living conditions are known to be relatively satisfactory; the food allowance for the *Malari* 1974 prisoners, for example, was 310 rupiahs (US $0.80) per day, which was better than the daily allowance for the 1965 prisoners (65 rupiahs a day), but was still inadequate. Some of the *Malari* 1974 prisoners, were allowed as much as 500 rupiahs (US $1.25) per day, depending on the prison, but this was exceptional (see Chapter 11).

When ordinary prisons previously intended for criminals are used, political prisoners are generally isolated from the other prisoners. The conditions of the untried political prisoners are far worse than those of convicted criminals.

The relatively few political prisoners who have been tried and sentenced are usually kept in prisons administered by civilian prison guards, for example, the prison at Cipinang near Jakarta.

The accommodation in prisons, except in a few such as Nirbaya and the RTM, is grossly inadequate, with extreme over-crowding. Sanitation and washing facilities are desperately poor. In some cases, prisoners who were issued with one bar of soap in 1971, have never since received another. Over-crowding in the prisons of the big cities has been eased somewhat by the transfer of political prisoners to prisons in smaller towns, but these smaller mixed prisons have totally inadequate facilities and are extremely over crowded.

Even so, the prevailing conditions in prisons are relatively better than those at interrogation centers, where prisoners sleep in very small unventilated rooms, or are crammed together along guarded corridors.

The combination of grossly inadequate food, deficient in proteins and vitamins, the extreme over-crowding and the lack of adequate medical care, has made tuberculosis endemic amongst prisoners. In almost every Indonesian prison known to Amnesty International, there are known cases of tuberculosis and cases of suspected tuberculosis. In the relatively better prisons, these are isolated cases, but in the extremely over-crowded prisons, where medical care is virtually non-existent, the disease affects more than half the prisoner population. Many other diseases are also common in the prisons, especially beri-beri, infections of the skin, gastro-intestinal diseases and chronic ailments caused by diet deficiencies. But the incidence of tuberculosis is the most significant demonstration of the cumulative effect of continual long-term deprivation and lack of care. In the worst prisons, more than half the prisoners have contracted tuberculosis.

The government provides the most rudimentary medical facilities in prisons, and prisoners who fall ill in most cases rely on what they themselves or their fellow prisoners receive from outside. If the illness requires a visit to a hospital, the prisoner, in most cases, has to cover the cost of transport and to pay bribes to guards. Many prisoners have no money and must therefore do without treatment, even when seriously ill. In the prisons which provide some elementary medical care, the doctors' visits are infrequent and irregular, and drugs prescribed by the doctor must be brought and paid for by relatives. Prisoners who have no relatives to visit them (and this applies to about 85% of them) have to rely upon an occasional dose of medicine from the inadequate stock of drugs kept in some prisons. Even drugs bought outside or donated by welfare organizations are stored in the prison office and liable to be used by the officers and guards.

The current food allowance of 65 rupiahs (US $0.17) a day has been seriously affected by inflation and food prices. The standard diet for political prisoners consists of one small serving of plain boiled rice a day, amounting to a few spoonfuls. In many prisons other starch substitutes, such as tapioca, are given to the prisoners in place of rice. The small amount of starch provided as the staple for each meal is supplemented by a minute piece of soyabean cake (*tempe* or *tahu*) and occasionally a small piece of fish. Fortunate prisoners who are visited by relatives, bringing them food, receive crucial additional protein and vitamins. They share this with other less fortunate fellow prisoners and so no individual prisoner receives sufficient. Nonetheless, supplementary food from relatives is an intrinsic part of the system of political imprisonment. Because of the persistent denial of adequate official provisions, the food and drugs brought by the comparatively few relatives who visit prisoners are essential in preserving the lives and health of political prisoners in general. Amnesty International has repeatedly stated that it is the government's duty, since it holds these citizens arbitrarily without trial, to ensure the health and welfare of the prisoners.

Apart from food and drugs, virtually every item the prisoners use is supplied by people outside. The government provides a small cell housing several prisoners, and the prisoners have to acquire their own bed, clothes, washing materials and other requirements. Prisoners in some centers are allowed to make small objects for sale, and they need to do this in order to earn the money to buy at least some basic necessities for themselves.

With variations depending on which local centers they are in, prisoners are permitted visits from relatives perhaps once a fortnight or once a month, and if families are allowed to bring food, they may do so once a week by leaving it at the prison office. Usually, a certain portion of the food is eaten by the prison authorities. The prisoners are denied writing materials, except in some prisons, where an occasional postcard to relatives, limited to 20 words, is permitted. No reading matter is allowed, except the Bible and the Koran.

Prisoners who belong to a particular religion may attend a weekly prayer meeting, which is conducted by a religious worker supervised by military chaplains, or by moslem *imams*. During the past year, there have been indications that *Kopkamtib* has forbidden the churches to make new converts among the prisoners, as the government is embarrassed because a large proportion of prisoners have become registered as converted Moslems, Roman Catholics and Protestants.

The prisons described below are selected partly because they are representative of a wide geographical area. A number of them are located in the most remote parts of Indonesia and are small and obscure. Nonetheless, there are hundreds of such small town jails holding political prisoners, and these have always been ignored by the Indonesian authorities when they present statistics about the total number of political prisoners.

Surakarta

The prison in the town of Surakarta in east-central Java is a typical prison of medium size, holding only untried political prisoners. There are altogether about 450 of them, 30 to 40 chronically ill and most of the time confined in separate buildings for sick prisoners. The prisoners themselves do not know to which category they have been assigned.

They are housed in four old buildings surrounded by a high wall. The cells within the buildings each contain a number of prisoners; a few are shared by two prisoners, while others are shared by more than 20. In each cell are raised cement platforms to serve as beds. The lavatory facilities are limited to a hole in the ground in each cell which is connected to the outside drain and is flushed with water kept in a container. There are also in addition, two rooms for prisoners receiving punishment.

The medical officer who is nominally supposed to visit the prison in fact does so only infrequently. In cases of emergency, prisoners are sent to a nearby hospital where any medical care they receive has to be paid for by them. More than a tenth of the prisoners are known to suffer from tuberculosis. Of the total of more than 450 prisoners, 190 need regular treatment for some illness or another.

The prisoners are given one meal a day, served just before noon and consisting of a small serving of rice and vegetable soup, together with a minute portion of *tempe* or *tahu*. Nothing else is provided. The prisoners' families are allowed to send in food.

The prisoners are allowed to make small handicrafts, which they sell, through their families, although they earn very little in this way. They are also required by the officials to work without payment outside the prison, for example, they have been required to construct a tennis court.

They may not read newspapers. The few books allowed are only religious ones. The permitted visits from their relatives may not exceed 10 minutes and are permitted once a fortnight.

This prison, compared with most others can be said to be relatively "adequate". Here the prisoners are treated somewhat better than is generally the case elsewhere. There have been no reported cases of brutality.

Bukit Duri

Bukit Duri Prison in Jakarta, the Indonesian capital, contains only women prisoners. According to the latest estimate, about 50 women are detained there. Most have been in prison for more than 11 years. It is believed that about 25 of them have been placed in category A and the remainder as category B. (There are other units which hold women political prisoners only, such as at Plantungan in Semarang in north-central Java, which holds about 300. Near Semarang is another women's prison at Bulu, which holds about 60 women political prisoners. In Malang in East Java, there is a prison holding eight women political prisoners in appalling conditions.)

Bukit Duri is another prison where the detainees are relatively better off than the majority elsewhere. The prison was once extremely over-crowded, but many prisoners were transferred to other prisons. Cells hold from one to four inmates. They sleep on cement bed platforms using mattresses and pillows that they or their relatives have supplied. A male army doctor visits the prison once a week and two of the prisoners help as nurses. Among the prisoners is a doctor, Mrs Sutanti, who is denied facilities to treat the other prisoners.

The daily meal is supposed to be taken about noon and consists of a little rice with *tempe* or *tahu*. This is supplemented by the prisoners by means of the small sums of money they earn from their handicrafts. The prisoners supply their own clothes, soap and washing materials. They take turns in cooking the prison food.

One incoming and one outgoing letter a month are supposed to be permitted. The prisoners have to ask the commandant for writing paper.

Each prisoner may have a monthly visit of half an hour. Up to three to five visitors are allowed per prisoner. About a tenth of the prisoners have relatives in the Jakarta area, but the families of the remainder live too far away for the journey to be feasible, or else there are no relatives who could visit. A visiting permit must be obtained from the military authorities and this has to be renewed every three months. Families may bring food to the prisoner and this has to be left at the prison gate. Although the current treatment of the prisoners does not appear to be particularly harsh, during their early years in detention some of them were interrogated and severely tortured. The husbands of many of the married women are also detained or have died, and the children of the more fortunate are looked after by relatives and other people. There are several confirmed and suspected tuberculosis cases.

The position of these prisoners is examined in greater detail in Chapter 10. It should, however, be stressed that physical conditions for these women are bearable only because of their own efforts to obtain their minimal requirements. As in the case of most other prisoners, the authorities provide inadequate food and other necessities.

Lampung

Lampung Prison is near the town of Tanjungkarang in the southernmost part of Sumatra. It is a mixed prison containing about 200 criminal prisoners, who are kept separate from the approximately 30 political prisoners. Of the latter, 15 are women. There are known to be two children aged five in prison with their mothers, who are political prisoners. Lampung is in many ways a typical small political detention center in a regional town. The political prisoners are kept in three cells, two for the women and one for the 16 men. Seven of the latter have to sleep on the ground. There is an open lavatory consisting of a hole in the ground in each cell connected to outside drainage. As is usual, the prison authorities provide no soap for personal washing and laundry.

An army doctor is supposed to be in charge of medical care for the prisoners, but he has never visited the prison. The prison authorities provide no medical facilities whatsoever. Twice a month, nurses from a religious social work organization visit the prisoners. Seven prisoners out of a total of 31 are confirmed tuberculosis cases. Several prisoners have other illnesses. Medicines are desperately needed.

The food provided by the prison authorities is quite inadequate. The daily ration amounts to only one bowl of cooked rice weighing about 300 grams. No protein in the form of meat or fish is provided except on four special days in the year. The only prisoners to receive vegetables are those who have earned some money from their handicrafts or have received help from their families.

In this way too the prisoners provide their own soap and clothing, none being provided by the authorities. The prisoners' families are poor and seldom able to supply any material necessities.

Although the prisoners are supposedly permitted regular visits from their families, it is very difficult for the latter to obtain permission to visit, and they are limited by the authorities to only a few visits a year. The isolation of the prisoners is so serious that their mental condition is reported to be seriously affected.

The confinement of infants with one of their parents in prison is not unusual.

Liananggang

The prison is in the village of Liananggang, which is 20 kilometers southeast of Banjarmasin in the southernmost part of Kalimantan (Indonesian Borneo). It is a prison exclusively for political detainees: 12 women, 4 boys and 7 girls, and about 140 men. The children, aged 2 to 11 are not classified as political detainees by the authorities, although they are held with their parents. The prison consists of eight buildings in open ground surrounded by barbed wire. The wooden buildings are thatched with palm leaves. The floors are beaten earth. There is no electric lighting.

The prisoners provide their own clothing and soap, and supplement their food ration with their earnings from raising poultry and from cultivation of pineapples and vegetables. From the sale of their produce, they each earn about 40 rupiahs (US $0.10) a day.

In general, the conditions in this prison resemble those in most prisons, except that the prisoners are allowed to keep poultry and that there are as many as 11 children in the prison. The older children are allowed to attend school in Liananggang; their families have to pay for this. There are no educational facilities for the younger children.

Ranomut

Ranomut prison is six kilometers from Manado, at the northernmost tip of the large island of Sulawesi (formerly known as The Celebes). The prison holds more than 300 political prisoners, of whom perhaps 60 are former police and military personnel and the remainder civilians. All the prisoners are category B.

The buildings are in open ground surrounded by a double row of barbed wire. The roofs have no internal ceilings and do not provide adequate protection from the heat. Not having blankets, most of the prisoners cover themselves at night with jute sacking material.

The prison authorities do not provide a visiting doctor, nor do they provide medicines. When seriously ill, prisoners are taken to a hospital in Manado. The prisoners have to pay for any drugs prescribed, and since most of them do not have the money with which to pay, the prescriptions are meaningless. The prisoners' families are extremely poor, having been deprived of their breadwinner and cannot give financial assistance with money. There are several cases of tuberculosis and other chronic diseases. Many of the prisoners need dental treatment, but none is allowed.

The daily food ration is a mash of rice and ground maize (less than 200 grams), with a minute piece of fish. The prisoners grow some vegetables with which to supplement their diet.

Although in theory prisoners are allowed visits from their families every third week, the commandant rarely grants permission.

The prisoners had been transferred to this camp from Manado Prison in 1973. When imprisoned in Manado from 1965–1973, at least 25 of them had died because of their privations. Their present condition, bad as it is, is relatively better than before 1973.

Payakumbuh

The prison is in the center of the town of Payakumbuh (population of about 60,000), 30 kilometers east of Bukit Tinggi in central Sumatra. It is a mixed prison containing about 50 political prisoners, one of them a woman who is kept in a cell with four criminal prisoners. Most of the prisoners have been in jail since 1965 and were tortured during interrogation, although there has been no more torture for the past two years. General conditions are bad and similar to those in most other Indonesian prisons.

There are several other political prisons in the Bukit Tinggi area, containing altogether about 1,500 prisoners.

Brief notes on a number of other typical prisons

Masohi is on the large island of Ceram in the Maluku archipelago (formerly known as The Moluccas). There is a camp here containing more than 80 prisoners.

At *Martapura,* 40 kilometers east of Banjarmasin in Kalimantan, there is a prison with 25 political detainees.

At *Soasiu* in Tidore Island, a relatively small island in north Malukum there are six political prisoners, two of whom are men, all imprisoned in a house near the local military commander's residence.

There is a prison in the town of *Ternate* on Ternate Island, which is relatively small and just north of Soasiu Island in the Malukus. It contains more than 200 male prisoners and 20 women prisoners, all of whom are category B. In general, conditions here are roughly equivalent to those elsewhere, except that some of the prisoners were required to build new houses for army officials outside Ternate and others have had to work in a fishery. The prison is very over-crowded.

At *Den Pasar* in Bali, there is a prison with more than 300 political prisoners.

At *Malang* in eastern Java there is a prison holding more than 590 political prisoners. More than 15% of the prisoners have died since 1966. They are frequently beaten by Lieutenant Suleiman, the deputy commandant, and by the guards, and the interrogations that are held are exceptionally brutal. Few families can afford to visit the prisoners.

The prison at *Ambarawa* in Central Java, holding about 910 prisoners, was once a Dutch colonial prison, and the prisoners' living conditions are at present extremely unhealthy. The prisoners are allowed very little food. Many of them are former soldiers including officers.

At *Kalisosok,* near Surabaya in East Java, conditions are also very bad. Among the 950 political prisoners there are several who were recently reported to have been brutally tortured. Brutal, continuous torture has been the norm at this notorious prison.

LABOUR CAMPS

Most untried political prisoners are liable to be used as forced labour and can be made to work in mines, on plantations, in fisheries and on building and public works projects. Some of these projects are run by state corporations and agencies, others by private companies with whom local commanders have a financial arrangement whereby they are paid a regular sum for each drafted prisoner, out of which a very small amount, sufficient to buy only cigarettes, and thus called "cigarette money", is given to the prisoner. Prisoners may be moved daily from their camps to a place of work; alternatively, they may be housed in temporary billets like that at Cilacap, where they are forced to work in an iron ore mining project, to which they were moved from Nusakambangan. Prisoners are also used by the local military to grow rice and vegetables and to raise livestock for the benefit of local army garrisons. They are also used as servants, as gardeners and as labourers, and in projects such as building houses and making tennis courts. For such work, they are usually given a minimal payment or nothing at all.

The trend of government policy increasingly has been to keep prisoners in camps which are located in farming country and to maintain a prison system which forces them to work as agricultural labourers. This is partly so that the prisoners' food ration can be supplied by the produce of their labour, and partly in order to supply the food for the officers and guards. This system enables the local military commanders to profit from the exploitation of prisoner labour. The following two examples illustrate how this forced labour system works.

Tanggerang

This prison is in the town of Tanggerang, which is 25 kilometers west of Jakarta. There are about 200 category B male prisoners. All are required to work in an adjacent prison farm, of more than 100 acres (40 hectares).

The prisoners are confined in buildings looking like an ordinary prison. They have to sleep on the ground on mats which they have themselves to supply. Almost all their necessities, such as cooking utensils, pillows and soap, have to be supplied by their families. Once a year, the prison authorities distribute a shirt and a pair of trousers to some prisoners, but not to others.

The food ration consists mainly of rice and vegetables. Sometimes *tempe* or *tahu* is provided, and, very occasionally, a little fish or meat, or an egg. The prisoners receive supplementary food from their families who have to leave it at the prison gates and may do so three times a week.

Inside the prison, the prisoners have to cook, clean and repair the buildings and to grow vegetables. The work outside the prison, called "the project", is on the prison farm and involves growing rice, raising fish in a fish farm, raising goats, buffaloes and poultry. This work is compulsory for all prisoners and the prisoners are not given any payment whatsoever. They may not use their own produce, that is they cannot eat any of the rice, fish or meat that they have produced, except when a very small portion of it is given them as part of their prison ration, which is quite insufficient and has to be supplemented by the food from their families.

The prisoners walk to the prison farm and start work from eight in the morning. They continue until 5 p.m. and have an hour's lunch break at noon.

They are not allowed to read newspapers or to listen to the radio. They are permitted 30-minute weekly visits, but only by close relatives.

Nusakambangan

Nusakambangan is a peninsula south of the port of Cilacap in south-central Java. Because it is separated from the mainland by a river, it is commonly referred to as an island. In the past, Nusakambangan had been notorious as a convict colony, housing criminal prisoners, and until recently the only people allowed on the island were convicts, political prisoners and their guards. The government is hoping to develop Nusakambangan as a nature reserve and tourist center, and the neighbouring port of Cilacap is the focus of major development projects involving iron ore mining and the construction of facilities for servicing super-tankers and distribution of petroleum products.

The more than 4,500 prisoners are confined in more than seven, possibly nine, units. They may all be category B prisoners. The prison camps are spaced at intervals along the 50 kilometers' width of Nusakambangan. The buildings are in an appalling state of disrepair. The prisoners sleep on mats on wooden platforms.

The authorities provide eating utensils in some of the units. On 17 August 1974, (National Day), a small bar of soap was issued to every prisoner; apart from that, the prisoners have received nothing with which to wash themselves or their clothing. Since 1971, they have been issued with two sets of clothing, consisting of shirt and trousers.

They may receive supplementary food from their families, who either bring it with them when they visit or else post it. These arrangements are virtually useless because of the isolation of Nusakambangan and the great distances separating the prisoners from their family homes. Visits are very expensive and difficult to arrange, and posting parcels is expensive; furthermore, they are sometimes lost in transit or are stolen by the guards.

Apart from the ill and the very old, all prisoners are forced to work. Each unit is surrounded by fields, created from dense tropical jungle by the prisoners and farmed by them. The prisoners have to work on rubber plantations and in forestry, to build roads, to cultivate rice, to do carpentry and to construct and repair buildings, to raise cattle, poultry and goats, to collect bird dropping deposits to use as fertilizer, to clean the camps, to perform services for their guards and officers by sewing and in other ways, to cook their own food, and to make handicrafts (musical instruments, toys and carvings), which are marketed by the authorities. They have to work all day, from early morning until five in the afternoon, with an hour's break at noon. They are not paid for their work; the profits go to the military administration.

The prison ration consists of rice and vegetables. The prisoners are not permitted to use their own produce, and are never allowed to eat meat or poultry. A little dried fish is occasionally allowed. Prisoners may supplement this inadequate diet by personally, during their spare-time growing vegetables, mainly sweet potatoes and cassava.

As at Tanggerang, the prisoners on Nusakambangan are kept in extremely poor conditions, considering the work they are compelled to do, for the benefit of the military authorities. They are ill fed, unpaid, inadequately clothed, have negligible washing facilities and totally inadequate medical facilities. They are not given medicine when they fall ill.

These prisoners are in many ways worse off than those at Tanggerang. Nusakambangan is remote from the main centers of population and the prisoners' families tend to live in other parts of Java, far away from the island. Visits are very difficult to arrange. First permission has to be obtained from the military authorities at Semarang, which is in north-central Java, more than 200 kilometers away. Next, the family has to travel to Cilacap to a special port at Wijayapura to seek further permission to see the prisoner. This request is passed on to the authorities in Nusakambangan, who then have to find out in which unit the prisoner is, and bring the prisoner over by boat to Wijayapura for a brief meeting with the family. A typical example of the difficulties involved is the case of a prisoner's wife who sold their only bed and other saleable belongings to collect enough money to visit her husband with their children. After obtaining the necessary permission at Semarang, she went down to Cilacap and waited for four days for the prisoner. Unfortunately, the authorities said they could not find him in time, and, her money having run out, she had to leave with her children without seeing her husband.

Although visits are usually permitted twice a month, the few families who do attempt to visit prisoners are obstructed at various levels of the military hierarchy and have to bribe them.

The only other contact which prisoners have with their families is through censored postcards which they are allowed to send each month, writing a maximum of 20 words on each card. The post is very slow. In their postcards the prisoners invariably ask for medicines and other requisites and, although these are sent when the families can afford to buy them, the latter never receive any acknowledgement of the parcels.

CONCLUSION

There are illegal places of detention, referred to in Indonesian as *tempat tahanan gelap,* whose existence is concealed from the community. Another kind of detention is that of making prisoners the servants of army commanders; thus a girl prisoner who was found to be good at English was made to live in the commandant's house and teach his children. Other prisoners have to act as servants in military garrisons, they constitute an unpaid compulsory labour force for the garrison's benefit providing for their needs. Some small groups of prisoners are to be found in dwelling houses that serve as detention centers, for instance, at Soasiu on Tidore island. This is common throughout the Republic. The most usual practice is for a handful of political prisoners to be held in a segregated part of ordinary criminal prisons in small towns throughout the Republic.

The prisons cited in this chapter are by no means the only ones of their kind in the same locality; thus Bukit Duri is the women's prison in the national capital, Jakarta, but there are other prisons in Jakarta such as Salemba, with more than 500 prisoners, the RTM with several hundred prisoners, Nirbaya with about 60 prisoners, an interrogation center at Jalan Tanah Abang with 80 prisoners and another interrogation center at Gunung Sahari with 50 prisoners, as well as the 200 prisoners at Tanggerang.

Similarly, as well as the prison at Liananggang, there is within the environs of the city at Bangarmasim, another prison center containing more than 150 prisoners. Further away, the prison at Ranomut in North Sulawesi is only six kilometers distant from the prison in Manado with another 160 prisoners.

In the city of Semarang in Central Java, there is a prison at Mlaten for 200 men, and a prison at Bulu for 60 women political prisoners; and prisoners are still interrogated and tortured in a private house in Jalan Dr Tjipto's, which is used as an interrogation center. At Plantungan, near Semarang there is another women's prison, with about 300 inmates.

Another example is at Mojokerto in East Java where there is a political prison for more than 120 prisoners and also a military police headquarters (No.82), containing 25 prisoners. Throughout the Republic, small- and medium-sized towns tend to have only one prison, the bigger towns tend to have several containing political prisoners, as well as interrogation centers; and prisoners are to be found in local military barracks and used as forced labour by private firms and in public works projects.

As can be seen from the above examples, prison conditions vary, as regards routine requirement to work, medical facilities, food rations and living conditions in general. Although there are great differences, clearly conditions on the whole are extremely poor, and they certainly do not conform to the standards said to be government policy and which the government claims are met. Prisoners mostly receive less than their daily food ration of 65 rupiahs, which anyway is insufficient. The prison guards tend to pilfer the little food which is intended for the prisoners. Moreover, it is common practice for the guards to consume much of the food which families bring for prisoners; as a rule therefore, families and welfare organizations bring food for the guards as well as food for the prisoners, in the hope that the foremen will allow the prisoners a certain amount of what has been brought for them.

Prisoners are subject to beatings. They are frequent and brutal in such prisons as Kalisosok, Ambarawa, Malang and others where the commandants themselves encourage cruelty or permit junior officers to torture prisoners. The Indonesian Government has the power to abolish torture.

9

TRANSPORTATION TO PENAL SETTLEMENTS: THE BURU SOLUTION

When the Indonesian Government announced on 1 December 1976 that it intended to release all category B prisoners in a phased program over three years, it also announced plans to transport prisoners to permanent settlements remote from their home areas. The Government's announcement implied that many prisoners would be "released" by being transported to penal settlements. The Chief of Staff of *Kopkamtib,* Admiral Sudomo, gave this explanation:

> "There must be sufficient employment opportunities for (category B prisoners), since unemployment would create fertile ground for all kinds of acts contrary to law, and this in itself would pose a threat to the national security, particularly to law and order. For this reason, the Government plans to establish transmigration centers in Sumatra, Kalimantan, Sulawesi and other places. Those who come from Java which is densely populated, are to be transmigrated to the island of Buru and other islands, in accordance with the guidelines on national transmigration as stated in the Second Five-Year National Development Plan. The program states that the resettlement and transmigration require a large budget and this could not be met in one fiscal year; hence the release by phases in 1977, 1978 and 1979." (Press statement released by the Indonesian Embassy, London, see Appendix II).

The Indonesian Government's tendency to think in terms of penal settlements for political prisoners has been evident for a number of years. Instead of releasing prisoners, the Government has conceived plans to remove them from their home provinces, transport them to penal settlements, and to explain such projects as "transmigration" in furtherance of national development schemes. In this way, the Government has hoped for several years to "solve" the problem of political prisoners.

The realities of the "transmigration solution" are illustrated by the experience of political prisoners who have been transported to the penal settlements on Buru Island. It may be recalled that even in the case of Nusakambangan (see Chapter 8), that the transfer of prisoners to the prison camps on that island, to some extent, resembled penal resettlement and forced labour. However, the Government's experiment on the island of Buru most clearly demonstrates the harshness of the "transmigration solution" and its gross violations of human rights. The prisoners removed from their prisons in Java to the harsh physical conditions of Buru are not allowed visits from their relatives and friends, and are all subject to compulsory labour.

THE BURU SCHEME

The island of Buru is part of M⸱'ıku, one of Indonesia's easterly groups of islands. It is mountainous and for the most part covered by dense primary jungle. There is an indigenous civilian population of about 40,000 living in coastal areas. Agricultural methods are primitive. The island has no roads linking the small capital Namlea to other townlets and villages; the only form of transportation is along rivers or beaten tracks. Regular communication with the rest of the Republic is virtually non-existent, the only link being an occasional transport service between Namlea and Ambon, the capital of Maluku. There are altogether more than 18 prison camps holding political detainees on the island.

In July 1969, the Indonesian Government announced the establishment of a permanent resettlement camp for untried political prisoners on Buru Island. By then the first batch of 2,500 prisoners had been transported there in conditions of utmost secrecy from prisons throughout Java. Until 1975, there were more than 9,800 prisoners on the island. This was significantly less than the total number of prisoners transported to Buru from July 1969, which amounted to more than 10,000.

Amnesty International received information in 1975 that the prisoners on Buru were compelled to construct new camps sufficient to house several thousand prisoners whom the authorities intended to transport to the island in 1976. It is now known that more than 4,000 prisoners have been transported to Buru in 1977, again in conditions of utmost secrecy. Thus, there are now about 14,000 prisoners held in camps on the island.

The authorities have reported the deaths of 143 prisoners during the first six years after they began to arrive on Buru, but certainly this is an underestimate. As regards the few individual cases for which the authorities have stated cause of death, the brief explanation, such as "intoxication", is insufficient to indicate whether the prisoner died from an illness, committed suicide or died from other causes. The suppression of adequate public information does not allay suspicion that the authorities are embarrassed about such a high death rate among prisoners said to have been chosen for transportation to Buru after they had been checked for physical fitness. It is still the case, as when the Buru "project" was started, that the physical conditions of the areas on the island allotted to the prisoners are exceptionally harsh.

The establishment of detention camps on Buru made political imprisonment more permanent. Instead of bringing the prisoners to trial and releasing those against whom no charges could be brought, the government had embarked on a course of long-term compulsory "resettlement" for the prisoners concerned.

The prisoners were transferred in secrecy and great haste from various prisons throughout the Republic where they had been relatively near to their families. In most cases there was no time for leave taking. They were transported by the ship *Tobelo* mainly in September 1969, December 1970 and throughout 1971. At Buru they were gathered together in a transit camp near Namlea, called Jiku Kecil, before being transferred to one of the units in the Apu Valley. At each site the prisoners were required to build a prison camp. They were made to build the bamboo rafts and carts for transportation along the river and jungle tracks.

The lands which are now cultivated fields were, in 1969, primary and secondary jungle. The prisoners had to clear the jungle and expand the areas under cultivation. At present, each unit of about 500 prisoners cultivates an area of between 50 and 300 hectares for rice, and up to 100 hectares for other crops such as maize, cassava and vegetables. Although there are large areas producing rice, the prisoners' food ration consists mainly of sweet potatoes, cassava and vegetables. Part of the rice stocks, timber and other products are used by the authorities, ostensibly for export to enable the purchase of fertilizer. It is now known that one third of the total produce resulting from prisoners' labour is seized by the military administration for the benefit of the officers and soldiers guarding the prisoners.

Indonesia ratified the International Convention on forced labour in 1950. The Report of the Committee of Experts of the International Labour Organization in 1976 affirmed that "the detainees cannot be considered to have offered themselves voluntarily for the work in question, but are performing forced or compulsory labour within the meaning of the Convention. The Committee trusts that measures will be taken at an early date to put an end to this situation".

The Indonesian Government immediately countered the ILO charge of using political prisoners for forced labour by reiterating

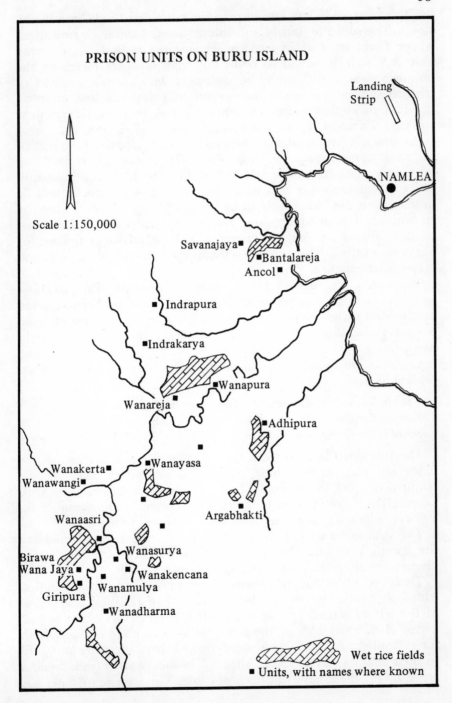

PRISON UNITS ON BURU ISLAND

Landing Strip

NAMLEA

Scale 1:150,000

Savanajaya■ Bantalareja
Ancol■

■ Indrapura

■Indrakarya

Wanapura
Wanareja

■Adhipura

Wanakerta■ ■Wanayasa
Wanawangi■

Argabhakti

Wanaasri

Birawa
Wana Jaya ■Wanasurya
Giripura Wanakencana
Wanamulya

■Wanadharma

Wet rice fields
■ Units, with names where known

its December 1976 announced program of releases and "transmigration". This did not satisfy the International Labour Organization, whose Committee of Experts, in its new report in 1977, declared that it "... feels bound to point out that, in order to ensure the observance of the Convention, detainees who are not brought to trial should be permitted once again to enjoy full and effective freedom of choice of employment. It hopes that the Government will take the necessary measures to this end".

At times, when food has been scarce, the prisoners have had to eat snakes, mice, rats and dogs. Prisoners are known to have dug up a cow or other animal which had died and had been buried, in order to eat the meat. Salt, sugar and other items which cannot be produced on the island have to be bought by the prisoners from the authorities. The prisoners raise poultry and sell these and the eggs to the officers and guards in order to have sufficient money for basic necessities. The prisoners themselves rarely eat an egg and very seldom chicken.

When they first arrived, the prisoners were issued with two shirts and two pairs of trousers; since then no clothing has been supplied by the authorities. Some parcels of clothing have been received from prisoners' families. Clothing and mosquito nets are desperately needed.

Prisoners are allowed only religious books. The Prosecutor General reportedly said:

"Some books are allowed but the prisoners have no time to read. During the day they are working in the fields and in the evening there is no electricity." (*Kompas*, 23 June 1975).

The prisoners have to work eight or nine hours a day in the rice fields and plantations. Those assigned to specialized tasks are not required to work in the fields. Ailing prisoners, including those with tuberculosis, have to work in the camps, washing, cleaning and cooking. The only exceptions are those who are too ill to move.

The authorities do not provide medicine for the diseases which are rife among prisoners. Tuberculosis, skin infection and alimentary diseases are not given proper medical treatment.

There is little contact between prisoners and their families. Although entitled to receive letters from their families, only a few of the letters actually reach them, often after delays of up to half a year. Less than 15% of the prisoners have received a parcel from their families. Prisoners may send only a regulation-size postcard to their families and no more. Although in theory visits from families are allowed, these have not been possible. Not a single prisoner has had a family visit since arrival on Buru. However, the authorities have encouraged the prisoners to bring their families to Buru, to ensure the permanence of the "resettlement" scheme.

In July 1972, 84 wives with their children were sent to join their prisoner husbands in Buru. A second group of 62 wives was sent in February 1974. In early 1975, another group of wives, mainly from the Jakarta area in Java, was taken to Buru. In addition, two other families were sent to Buru, but when the authorities were unable to trace the husbands, the wives and children were returned to Java. The remaining wives, their husbands and their children are housed in a special camp called Savana-Jaya (Camp No.4). Altogether there are now about 400 children in the camp. Wives and children have to live under the same conditions as the prisoners and have to work for their food and basic requirements, except that the children are permitted to attend the elementary school in Namlea.

PERMANENT "RESETTLEMENT"

The decision to establish the Buru project was taken by *Kopkamtib,* and the Prosecutor General was appointed to supervise the project. Thus the military authorities which staff *Kopkamtib* delegated to the Prosecutor General's office the responsibility for those political prisoners whom it was official policy not to release. This, however, did not place the political prisoners on Buru in the control of civilian authority. The regional military command at Ambon is in charge of all security arrangements of the project and the guards are recruited from the Military Police Corps. Moreover, the Army is powerfully represented in *Bapreru* (Buru Resettlement Executive Authority), the executive chief of which is the commander of the 15th Military Command, based at Ambon, Brigadier General Abdul Rahman Suwodo.

The official reasons for the scheme were set forth by the then Prosecutor General, Sugih Arto, (himself a general), in the preface to a brochure issued by *Bapreru* in December 1969. This explained that the transfer of category B prisoners to Buru was intended "not to isolate them from the general public, but merely to provide them with a new way of living together with their families, because if they were to be returned to their original community now, their safety would be at risk". This explanation implies that the prisoners were transported to Buru for their own protection, but it is made clear in the very next sentence of the brochure that the underlying reasons for the policy were different: the Prosecutor General stated that the men sent to Buru were those who the government firmly believed had played "an important role in planning, supervising and carrying out. . . . the 30 September/PKI Movement either before, during or after it took place; however, we have not sufficient evidence to prosecute them further. We consider it still to be a danger to our security to return them to the community; they are still like a thorn in the side of the community". Thus it seemed to have been the government's view that it was the community which needed protection from people who could not be prosecuted because of lack of evidence.

The most striking thing about the Buru project is that those permanently detained there are compelled to labour for their own sustenance, thereby relieving the government of its responsibility to provide for the essential needs of people whom it detains without trial. Provisioning the prisoners on Buru was supposedly the authorities' responsibility only for the first eight months after their arrival; from then on the prisoners were forced to live from their own labour, but even then they were deprived of benefiting from the food they themselves produced. Official statements about Buru have always stressed that the project was not supposed to be a concentration camp, but an agricultural resettlement scheme, whereby political prisoners would be "given the opportunity" to become self-sufficient. The government insists that there is no forced labour on Buru. The Prosecutor General, in the *Bapreru* brochure, emphasized that "resettlement on Buru Island is not like any previous or recent concentration camps abroad because on Buru Island there is no forced labour".

The *Bapreru* brochure justifies the system of forced labour on humanitarian grounds. It refers to a Dutch colonial regulation stating that detainees should "whenever possible be given the opportunity to work". It then states that, according to Indonesian *Panca Sila* principles, "everyone, whether a member of a free society or undergoing punishment. . . is obliged to work". Such "principles" are the basis of the government's policy of forcing prisoners to work on Buru Island, and elsewhere, for instance in the prison camp at Tanggerang, and in labour camps on Nusakambangan. These principles are also used to justify the arbitrary employment of political prisoners throughout the Republic in forced labour projects. This view of the government is stated most clearly in the *Bapreru* brochure:

> "Procuring work for the detainees of the 30th September/PKI Movement, therefore, is one of the government's efforts to respect them as human beings who, in the interest of their physical and social development, must work to the best of their ability."

It is quite reasonable for the laws of any society to uphold the right of its free citizens to work; but it is surely wrong for a government to assume the right to compel untried detainees to work in order to survive. The survival of political prisoners on Buru depends on their doing a long day's arduous labour under the strict supervision of armed guards. It is a program that applies to all, the young and the old, the sick and the healthy, except for those who are so ill that they cannot rise from their sleeping mats. One foreign journalist who visited the island in December 1971 reports in *Newsweek*, 14 February 1972:

"For those with no previous farming experience, and for the older men and the intellectuals, the gruelling manual labour is sheer physical punishment."

Forced labour is performed by men for whom the government no longer considers itself responsible. They are forced to engage in hard labour while weak from prolonged food deprivation. A high proportion of the prisoners are chronically ill but do not receive even the most elementary medical treatment. They are without adequate clothes and other requisites. Although the majority are unfit for hard physical labour yet they are compelled to perform this day after day.

In 1972, when it was first learnt that there was a high death rate on Buru, officially admitted to be 143, the authorities explained that the prisoners had died not because of conditions on Buru, but as a result of ailments they had before their transfer. Yet it was emphasized in the *Bapreru* brochure that all prisoners transferred to Buru had undergone medical examinations to check their physical fitness. By December 1972, the Indonesian Embassy in London was claiming that deaths were due not to illness but to old age; this contradicted the original assertions that no one aged over 45 was to be transported to the island.

FAMILIES ON BURU

The Indonesian authorities have always insisted that their plans to bring the families of the Buru prisoners to the island are humane. But the prisoners themselves, and most of their relatives regard the matter very differently. In December 1971, when a group of Indonesian and foreign journalists visited Buru, not a single prisoner to whom they spoke showed any desire to have his family with him. While separation from their families is one of the most intolerable aspects of their existence, they realize that life on Buru is totally unacceptable to and far too arduous for their wives and children.

In a speech to foreign journalists in Jakarta in December 1971, the Prosecutor General admitted that a survey of the attitudes of wives towards the prospects of joining their husbands in Buru, had shown that 75% were unwilling to do so, particularly because of problems with regard to their children. Despite this, the government proceeded with its plans and the first 84 families reached the island in July 1972.

That October, the senior army commander then in charge of Buru, Brigadier General Wadli Prawirasupradja, told a press conference in Jakarta that by the end of 1972, 4,500 family members would have been transported to the island, and that eventually all the prisoners' families would join their husbands or fathers, raising the total population of the camp to 50,000 (including prison officers and guards). At the same press conference, the Prosecutor General made it clear that, although the families were free citizens, they would not be allowed to leave "the project" once they had arrived on Buru. He admitted too, that enormous social problems had arisen as a result of the arrival of the families. He mentioned the following:

— education of the children: if this were left to the parents, the children might grow up "dedicated communists", he said;

— contact with the outside world: this could not be freely permitted as it could be a channel for "subversive activities";

— the families' livelihood: they could not be provided for indefinitely by the government; yet to allow them to earn a livelihood would lead to the use of money, and he was afraid that if there were "too much money" in the hands of the families it would be used for "subversive activities".

A second group of 62 families was transported to Buru in February 1974. In early 1975, more families (about 49 dependants) were sent to the island. Despite continuing government pressure to make families go to Buru, the total number on the island is less than 200, and this reflects the refusal of the prisoners and their wives to accept the government's project at face value. It is clear that wives and children transported to the island are deprived of their ordinary liberties and suffer prison restrictions in No.4 camp at Savana-Jaya. Neither wives nor children are allowed to leave the island, and they have to endure the harsh conditions imposed on the prisoners. In its issue of 21 October 1972, the Indonesian weekly *Tempo* commented:

"People can well say that, having brought the families there, [to Buru], the problem of the political prisoners appears to have become more complicated than before."

In March 1976, the Deputy Commander of *Kopkamtib*, Admiral Sudomo, in an interview published in *Tempo,* said that the families were being sent to Buru so that the prisoners "will feel more at home". Amnesty International, however, continues to receive letters from prisoners' wives, which suggest otherwise. One wife said:

"We are being compelled to fill in forms agreeing to go there too. I filled in the form, saying 'not willing', but it seems they are going to force us to go to Buru."

RETURN TO SOCIETY

According to a December 1971 statement, by the then Deputy Prosecutor General, Sutrisno Hamidjojo, who was in charge of the Buru project, the final stage for Buru prisoners is when they are "returned to society". The phrase "returned to society" seems to imply rehabilitation or release, in other words, the end of detention. But the Indonesian authorities had a different idea in mind. At this stage, said the Deputy Prosecutor General:

"Political prisoners would remain on the island but would no longer be bound by discipline, such as, having to attend roll-call."

As with prisoners elsewhere in the Republic, the authorities have stated that political prisoners would be considered rehabilitated when they had changed their ideology from communism to *Panca Sila.* The authorities, however, do not specify by exactly what criteria their prisoners' ideological tendencies could be verified, especially when they consider the latter "dedicated communists" and "traitors". Up till the present, the government has clearly not taken the trouble to spell out a release programme whereby the prisoners could spend the rest of their lives as free citizens of the Republic. This applies on Buru to both old and young men (some of whom were under 15 when arrested). A case in point is the boy who was transported to the island with his only parent, his father, who was a political prisoner. The father died in captivity but his son is still on the island. The future is bleak also for those wives and children on the island who are now the permanent inhabitants of a prisoner colony.

The wife of a prisoner on Buru wrote recently to Amnesty International:

"Now he is still there, far from his wife and family. Where is the humanity of our country?"

The London *Daily Telegraph* interviewed a prisoner on Buru in March 1972. The reporter asked the prisoner: "Are you happy in Buru?" He replied: "Of course, no, no." The reporter continued: "The Government says that you are happy." The prisoner replied: "Of course, yes, yes. What else will they say?"

GOVERNMENT POLICY

The Indonesian Government speaks of prisoners being "transmigrated to the island of Buru and other islands, in accordance with the guidelines on national transmigration as set forth in the Second Five-Year National Development Plan". The impression given is that the prisoners are being treated in the same way as ordinary Indonesian citizens who voluntarily transmigrate to other islands. Clearly the Buru project is completely different from what the Government means by national "transmigration" in relation to free citizens of the Republic.

The main characteristics of the Buru project are quite clear. First, those affected were long-standing political prisoners held without trial when they were transported to Buru, and they have remained prisoners there. The Government has cajoled and threatened families to join the prisoners in prison camps on the island, but the majority of the families have resisted attempts to transport them to the island. Not a single prisoner has ever been "released" on the island, and not a single prisoner or member of his family who has joined him on the island, has been allowed to leave Buru. The Buru project, simply, means the transportation of political prisoners to a permanent penal colony.

Moreover, the prisoners are systematically used as forced labour, are made to supply all the food and necessities for their very survival, and are compelled even to provide the food consumed by the Army officials guarding them.

Transportation to a penal settlement, forced labour and exploitation, a desperate daily struggle for survival, permanent detention, these are the fundamentals of the Buru project.

Amnesty International has consistently opposed the Indonesian Government's Buru project. The Buru "solution" is a totally deplorable model for the Indonesian Government to use when formulating plans to "transmigrate" other untried political prisoners to Buru and other islands. When the Indonesian Government talks about "releases", they should mean the proper and unconditional release of prisoners, and not the "transmigration solution".

The prisoners' predicament was clearly conveyed by the Indonesian journalist, Marcel Beding, in the Indonesian newspaper,

Kompas, after his visit to Buru in December 1971:

"How long have they to stay there [in Buru]? They themselves are asking this question. Their families are asking this question and I myself join in asking it. And the answer is as dark as the sky above Unit 2 on that December afternoon in 1971. . . . They are all lonely men. They are all lonely while labouring from morning to sunset. They are also troubled by the feeling of uncertainty about the future and about their loved ones far across the sea, parents, wives, children, relatives."

10

WOMEN AND IMPRISONMENT

President Suharto's "New Order" banned *Gerwani* (*Gerakan Wanita Indonesia*: Indonesian Women's Movement) and a large number of mass organizations for alleged complicity in the abortive coup.

Gerwani was by that time the largest women's organization in Indonesia, with a membership of more than one million. It was not officially affiliated to the Communist Party, but described itself as "an organization of communist and non-communist women". It was part of the left-wing movement quashed by the military as soon as the attempted coup had been foiled. Compared with other organizations, *Gerwani* was singled out for attack in the anti-left campaign. Sensational allegations were made about it which played a large part in provoking massacres that occured in many parts of the country during the last three months of 1965 and in 1966. To explain this, also to explain the circumstances of the arrest of a number of women still in detention, it is necessary to refer briefly to the events of 1 October 1965.

The coup conspirators established their headquarters at a paramilitary training camp in Lubang Buaya, located on an Air Force base on the outskirts of Jakarta. This training camp had been used for several months to train volunteers for "Confrontation" with Malaysia. Political parties and organizations supporting President Sukarno and his confrontation policy responded to a call for volunteers by setting up their own training camps. The camp at Lubang Buaya was being used by several nationalist and left-wing organizations. A number of women and girls had attended courses there from the middle of 1965 till the day of the attempted coup. In addition to those attending para-military courses, there were women helping with health services and performing kitchen and dormitory duties.

During the coup attempt by middle-ranking Army officers, six generals were kidnapped and killed, and their bodies were found in a disused well at Lubang Buaya. After the bodies were discovered, sensational reports appeared in the press alleging that their sex organs had been mutilated and eyes gouged out. It was further alleged that these atrocities had been committed by the women at the camp. The women were said to have engaged in obscene dancing and to have prostituted themselves in a grotesque manner.

President Sukarno, still formally Head of State but rapidly losing political control, ordered a post mortem examination of the bodies and this revealed that there had been no mutilation. Eyes were damaged because the bodies had been immersed in water. The stories persisted however, and newspapers published reports of confessions made by young girls during interrogation by military officers.

Underlying these sensational reports, which had a traumatic effect on Indonesian society, was a story of torture and sexual abuse of these girls under interrogation, many of whom were politically naive and terrified into making confessions by the torture and abuse to which they were subjected.

Gerwani was accused by the authorities of having mobilised these girls and of being responsible for the alleged atrocities. Yet despite the shrillness of these accusations, it is a fact that even now, more than 11 years after the event, no one alleged to have been directly involved in the Lubang Buaya events has been tried. So far only a handful of women have been brought to trial, and the charges against them were not directly related to the alleged atrocities in Lubang Buaya. Approximately 800 trials have so far taken place, many of them related to actual occurences in Lubang Buaya, but the alleged atrocities have never been confirmed by the testimony of witnesses who appeared at these trials. Hundreds of women and girls said to have been responsible for or indirectly involved in the events, are still held in prison, without charge or trial.

The first major trial of women prisoners began nine years after the 1965 events, in February 1975 (see Chapter 6).

WOMEN PRISONERS

It is not possible to establish precisely how many women are still being held without trial. The largest womens' prison is at Plantungan in Central Java where there are about 300 inmates. About 50 women are detained in Bukit Duri prison in Jakarta and about 60 in the women's prison in Bulu near Semarang. There are women's prisons throughout the archipelego. Probably about 2,000 women are being held without trial.

Gerwani leaders and members probably comprise a fairly large proportion of the women prisoners. Many members of the organization's central board are known to be in detention as well as local members. *Gerwani* members were persecuted during the first few days after the abortive coup. Many hid, often by moving to other areas. Reports of the "discovery" of such "fugitives from justice" still appear in the Indonesian press. There must be many thousands of women in Indonesia who, lest they get arrested, are still striving to conceal their past legitimate membership of previously public, and respectable organizations.

A Typical Case: Mrs Sundari

Mrs Sundari was active in her local branch of *Gerwani* in Jakarta at the time of the abortive coup. Her husband was also a member of a left-wing organization. Their home was a center of political activity and various political groups held meetings there. Shortly after the coup attempt, an Army team raided their house. They claimed that a meeting had taken place there shortly before the coup and that political plans had been made at that meeting. The Sundaris were probably suspected of discussing possible political developments in the event of a left-wing takeover. Such a suspicion would have been enough to get them arrested on accusations of direct involvement in the attempted coup. Both Mrs Sundari and her husband were arrested in October 1965. She has been in Bukit Duri Prison ever since and she is one of the 14,000 prisoners on Buru Island.

WOMEN AT LUBANG BUAYA

Women who were at Lubang Buaya or who were alleged to have been there also comprise a considerable proportion of the prisoners. Many of them were girls in their early teens when arrested in 1965. A number of them are illiterate.

A Typical Case: Walmijati

At the time of the attempted coup, Walmijati was an auxilary in the Friendship Hospital, Jakarta. She was about 15 at the time. While working in Jakarta, she attended training courses at the Lubang Buaya camp. It is not known exactly what her political affiliations were, but she probably belonged to one of the youth movements that went to Lubang Buaya for training.

During interrogations, Walmijati was severely beaten and injured. She denied accusations that she had participated in the alleged sexual atrocities at Lubang Buaya. After the beatings by the interrogators, she became emotionally disturbed. She was arrested in October 1965 and detained in Bukit Duri Prison. She has been there ever since and has not been tried. Her family is poor and cannot afford to visit her in prison.

TRADE UNIONISTS

There are also activists among the prisoners. Women workers had for many years played a prominent part in the trade union movement.

The left-wing trade union federation, SOBSI, had an active Women's Department, many of whose members are now in prison.

A Typical Case: Mrs Pudjiati

Mrs Pudjiati is about 50. She was born in Central Java and since her youth has been involved in left-wing movements in Indonesia. During the Japanese occupation and the war of liberation against the Dutch, she was a member of *Pesindo,* the Indonesian Socialist Youth, which later became *Pemuda Rakjat,* the People's Youth Movement. She worked for many years at the Unilever factory in Jakarta and while there, became involved in trade union activity. She was a well-known activist in SB Unilever (the trade union in the factory) and was several times arrested during demonstrations against rising prices and while on deputations calling for higher wages, These arrests took place while President Sukarno was in power. Pudjiati was also a member of the Jakarta Council of SOBSI, to which SB Unilever was affiliated.

After the abortive coup, many trade unionists were dismissed from their jobs. *SOBSI* and its affiliated trade unions were banned and many union members arrested. Their arrest and detention was because they belong to left-wing organizations and not because they were in any way involved personally in the coup. Pudjiati probably was arrested in 1966. She was detained in Bukit Duri Prison then transferred to Plantungan in 1971. She was transferred again in 1976 to Bulu Prison.

OTHER CASES OF WOMEN IN PRISON

Many of the women in prison were, however, simply victims of circumstance, people picked up on the streets unable to identify themselves or defend themselves against political charges; women whose sons and daughters were being sought by the Army; women who were picked up together with their husbands or brothers simply because they were relatives.

Two Typical Cases: Miss Tumirah

Miss Tumirah is in her mid-30s. She is not an educated woman and is uninterested in politics. At the time of the coup, she was doing domestic work or selling in markets. She was apparently picked up by the military simply because she failed to produce an identity card. Her case exemplifies the indiscriminate way in which arrests were made and the extremely inadequate arrangements for the quick release of people against whom no charge could possibly be made. She was arrested in the late 1960s and detained in Bukit Duri Prison. She has now been released.

Suhasih Suwardi

She was arrested, together with a friend, in 1969 when they went to the Army security authorities to make inquiries about their husbands who had been arrested. They were taken by the authorities to Bukit Duri Prison, where they have been kept ever since. Suhasih's husband is said to have given asylum to someone the authorities were looking for in connection with the attempted coup. He was arrested and tried on these charges and is now serving a 12 year sentence. Suhasih was presumably arrested because it was thought that she knew that her husband had given asylum to this man and that she had not reported him to the authorities for doing so.

GENERAL CONDITIONS

Some Indonesian prisons are exclusively for women, for instance, Bukit Duri (see also chapter 7). In some, women are used as forced labour, for instance, Plantungan. There are local prisons where young children live with their mothers, for instance, Lampung. In addition, there are the women (and their children) who have gone to Buru to joint their husbands, who now have to stay in special camps and may not leave Buru.

In general, women prisoners' conditions are much the same as men's, although where they are allowed to sell handicrafts and receive the returns for their work, their position is somewhat alleviated.

A number of the women prisoners have husbands who are also in detention. The major concern of a prisoner is the fate of his or her family and this concern is inevitably greater when both parents are in prison. Many women prisoners suffer the hardship of separation from their children. In many cases women have lost all contact with both husbands and children. No prisoners are permitted to initiate contact with their families; contact is made only if the family outside takes the initiative, and when both parents are in prison this is much less likely to happen.

Some women have the comfort of knowing their children are being cared for by relatives or neighbours, but this is not always the case. Even close relatives have been reluctant to look after the children of political prisoners because of the risks involved, social stigma and harassment.

TORTURE

Many women now in detention are known to have suffered severe torture during their interrogations by military intelligence officers.

The tortures inflicted have included beatings, attacks with knives or daggers, burning with cigarettes, sexual assault and electric shocks. The young girls arrested in connection with the events in Lubang Buaya were badly tortured and some of them have been permanently affected.

A torture case

The London *Sunday Times*, 11 January 1976, published an interview with a girl who had been a member of a left-wing organization before the coup and who was arrested in 1968. She was taken to the local military post and witnessed the torture of other women. She was herself severely tortured. She was stripped naked and then beaten with a stick by the intelligence officer. Her hair was burnt. Then she was placed on a table. A stick was inserted into her vagina and her pubic hair was burnt.

PRISONERS' FAMILIES

The wives and children of political detainees face enormous difficulties in a society that has become terrified of being suspected of personal acquaintance with political prisoners who have been so severely condemned by the Indonesian authorities. In normal circumstances, the strong sense of family responsibility overrides this; but political prisoners are beyond the pale, having for years been officially condemned.

"Certificates of Non-involvement" in the October 1965 events have, for many years, been the prerequisite for entering schools, obtaining employment and moving from one district to another. Even today, although the authorities have announced that such certificates are no longer required, the situation remains basically the same in most localities where central government policy is subject to the discretion of local military commanders and officials. Foreign firms are known to have to ask for such certificates when interviewing potential employees.

Few Indonesian women have regular employment or special occupational skills. Many prisoners' wives have tried to survive by selling cakes, dressmaking and setting up stalls, or have become domestic servants. But none of these forms of livelihood are very remunerative and the families have remained in a state of penury. Those who know where their husbands are detained take food to the prison, as they know what the conditions inside are like; this adds to their considerable financial burden. Another major expense is school fees and other educational expenses for their children. The state does not provide free primary or secondary education.

On top of having to cope with financial hardship, the prisoners' wives face suspicion and sometimes open hostility from their local communities. This has been largely due to government persecution of the prisoners and their families. The complex of difficulties experienced by prisoners' wives has had such severe effect that many have had to conceal their marriages or divorce their husbands.

11

THE MALARI AFFAIR

President Suharto's Government has detained people in connection with events other than those of 1965. The way these other prisoners have been treated shows that government policy and practice have been equally repressive as regards prisoners whom the authorities could not, and did not, claim to be communist.

Extensive rioting broke out in Jakarta on 15 January 1974, in the course of which 13 people were killed and 770 arrested. The Indonesian Government claimed that the *Malari* (15 January) Affair was a conspiracy to overthrow the Government, organized by two political parties which had been banned by the former President Sukarno in 1960, the *Parti Sosialis Indonesia* (PSI: Indonesian Socialist Party) and *Masjumi* (the leading Islamic party). President Suharto removed from key positions the three most important military figures in the country—Lieutenant General Ali Murtopo, General Sumitro and Lieutenant General Sutopo Juwono—implying that there was a power struggle within the military. It was following the dismissal of General Sumitro that President Suharto resumed the position of chief of *Kopkamtib*. General Sumitro was also relieved of his post of deputy commander of the Armed Forces.

The *Malari* incidents began with student demonstrations against the visit to Jakarta of the then Japanese Prime Minister. Subsequently there were extensive riots involving large numbers of people, which seemed to have been a reflection of widespread discontent with Government economic policy.

Most the 770 people arrested were accused of vandalism and looting. Five months after the *Malari* Affair, about 50 people remained in prison in Jakarta and another 32 in Surabaya. They were alleged to have instigated the riot. This alleged "hard core" of the *Malari* prisoners included distinguished former politicians, such as Mr Soebadio Sastrosatomo, leader of the PSI before it was banned in 1960; former chief advisers to President Suharto's Government, such as Professor Sarbini Sumowinata; important university lecturers, such as Dr Dorodjatan Kuntjorojakti; prominent human rights figures and lawyers, such as Mr Adnan Buyung Nasution and Mr Yap Thiam Hien; and university student leaders. The cases of all of them were taken up by Amnesty International.

Eleven months after his arrest, the student leader, Hariman

Siregar, was the first *Malari* defendant to be brought to trial. Subsequently, two other student leaders, Sjahrir and Aini Chalid, were also tried. The prosecution sought to establish that they were the ring-leaders of the *Malari* Affair, but none of the evidence produced in court proved that any of the student leaders were personally responsible for the *Malari* riots. Instead, it was clear that the three student leaders were responsible for criticizing the government's development policies, during the period immediately preceding the *Malari* Affair. The ultimate responsibility for the *Malari* riots, according to the three defendants, lay elsewhere. The question of who was responsible was not resolved at the trials, and there is still speculation in Jakarta about the extent to which the *Malari* Affair was an open manifestation of a power struggle within the military.

Eventually, in May 1976, more than two years after the *Malari* Affair, all the prisoners, except the three who had been tried, were released without trial. When the Prosecutor General, General Ali Said, told journalists that on 10 May 1976, that they had been released, he added that the state intelligence agency was continuing its investigation of those responsible for the *Malari* riots. "So far we have not found who they are, but the investigation is going on", he said. (*Indonesia Times*, 11 May 1976)

This statement prompted an instant response from Mr Adnan Buyung Nasution, Director of the Jakarta Legal Aid Institute, who had himself been a *Malari* prisoner held without trial. He pointed out:

> "The Prosecutor General's statement means that it is certain the champions and mastermind of *Malari* are not those people who were detained, because they were suspected of being the mastermind or ring-leaders of that incident, including myself and my friends. . .". (*Sinar Harapan*, 11 May 1976).

Of the three *Malari* prisoners who had been tried and who remained in prison, one was released in August and another in October 1976. Sjahrir, a former student leader at the University of Indonesia in Jakarta, is the last remaining *Malari* prisoner, serving a 6½ years' sentence.

These cases of imprisonment on charges of subversion illustrate the way in which the Indonesian authorities use the Subversion Act against political prisoners who were not held in connection with the 1965 attempted coup. Although detention without trial under the Subversion Act is limited to one year, nevertheless all the *Malari* prisoners held for more than a year were simply charged again under its provisions. This extended beyond one year their period of detention without trial. Moreover, it is now abundantly clear that the authorities had no case against people such as Buyung Nasution, who was detained for 22 months without trial, nor against other *Malari* prisoners who were held for up to almost two and a half years without trial. The trials of the student leaders were political show trials intended to camouflage the Government's embarrassment over widespread criticism of failures in its development programmes and the unrest in Jakarta which led to the riots.

The Government's handling of the *Malari* Affair illustrates its arbitrary way of treating those it considers its political opponents and those who criticise its policies. Immediately after the *Malari* Affair, the Government banned 11 newspapers and journals, including the country's oldest and most respected newspapers, *Indonesian Raya, Pedoman, Abadi, Harian Kami*. The authorities would not let former editorial staff members of these papers work on other publications. Thus Rosihan Anwar, a president of the Indonesian Journalist's Association, has not been allowed to work as a journalist since the closure of *Pedoman,* the paper he edited. The distinguished Indonesian journalist Mochtar Lubis was arrested, the official explanation for this being that the purpose of the arrest was "to find out his possible involvement" in the *Malari* Affair.

Significantly, among the people arrested were those who had strongly criticized the former regime of President Sukarno and who had been victimized by that government. They included Adnan Buyung Nasution, Professor Sarbini, and Mochtar Lubis. Mochtar Lubis was imprisoned for more than nine years by the Sukarno regime because of his exposure of political and administrative malpractices, and he was one of the Indonesian prisoners of conscience adopted by Amnesty International before 1965.

As well as imprisoning people without trial, the government also revealed how it dealt with those it regarded as dissidents. For example, Dr Deliar Noer, who received his doctorate at Cornell University in the United States, was, in 1966, a member of President Suharto's personal political advisory staff. At the time of the *Malari* Affair, he was president of the Jakarta Teachers' College, and was believed by the Government to have harboured "independent ideas". As a result he was barred from "teaching at any university"—state or private.

Then there is the case of Dr Soedjatmoko, former Indonesian ambassador to the United States. Although at the time of the *Malari* Affair he was special adviser to the Indonesian Planning Agency, *Bappenas,* Dr Soedjatmoko was banned from travelling outside the country, despite his long-standing links with organizations such as the Ford Foundation. The Indonesian security authorities suspected that Dr Soedjatmoko was one of the "brains" behind the *Malari* Affair, and he was subjected to intensive interrogation for three weeks.

None of the *Malari* prisoners were said by the government to have been communists, nor were they said to have been influenced by communists. Nonetheless, they remained in prison, in some cases for almost two and a half years without trial, and their detention would have lasted much longer had the Indonesian Government not been subjected to very strong international criticism. The Government asserted, when the *Malari* arrests took place, that the detainees were personally involved in the *Malari* Affair. This, the Indonesian Government has signally failed to prove. Similarly, as regards those political prisoners who were arrested and imprisoned for alleged "personal involvement" in the 1965 attempted coup, the Indonesian Government has not proved that those held without trial were personally responsible.

12

GOVERNMENT: SOCIAL POLICY
AND IMPRISONMENT

President Suharto's "New Order" has conducted an inquisition among Indonesians suspected of left-wing tendencies. The effects of the inquisition are widespread. First, there are the more than 5,000 prisoners, perhaps as many as 100,000 who are still held in grim conditions without trial. The damage done to the prisoners' families has been appalling. They have been victimized and denied employment. Moreover, the Indonesian Government has systematically denied employment in government and state departments to people suspected of leftist tendencies. Released prisoners are similarly denied access to government jobs; moreover, private firms in Indonesia are discouraged by the military authorities from employing released prisoners. The same applies to those not issued with a "Certificate of Non-involvement" which all Indonesians must possess in order to prove they were never subjected to the inquisition.

All this clearly shows why the situation of political prisoners is especially desperate. All "released" prisoners have to spend a year or more under "town arrest", which means that they must report regularly to specified military offices, and must apply for permission to leave a specified town; such permission is almost invariably refused. Moreover, a prisoner has to have a known, fixed address; this is a pre-condition of release, and it poses an insuperable problem for many prisoners whose family lives have been destroyed as a consequence of their more than 11 years' imprisonment, or because they find it difficult to trace their families. Many released prisoners, as well as being put under "town arrest" are also subjected to "house arrest", which means that they cannot leave their homes for several months and often for up to a year.

Because of these aspects of government policy, released prisoners are in an especially vulnerable position. Their families have been deprived of their financial support during their years of captivity. Following release, the prisoners are denied employment and this imposes an additional strain on the families' limited resources. Released prisoners retain the category to which the authorities have assigned them, and are thus labelled by the Government as constant suspects, even though released.

It is not surprising therefore that the friends, former acquaintances and neighbours of released prisoners are apprehensive about them and regard associating with them as dangerous and likely to attract the attention of *Kopkamtib*. For most ordinary Indonesians, a released prisoner is, in this sense, a dangerous person to know. And it is largely government policy as regards prisoners and their release which is the basis for this fear. A few exceptional Indonesians are prepared to express their opinions about the treatment of political prisoners.

The distinguished Indonesian lawyers, Mr Yap Thiam Hien and Mr Adnan Buyung Nasution, both of whom have been political prisoners themselves, have spoken out against the continued imprisonment and treatment of the prisoners held in connection with the 1965 events. In many cases, leading Indonesians would have expressed their views had they known about the true circumstances affecting political prisoners. There is widespread ignorance about the problem in Indonesia, despite the scale and depth of its effect on society. The ignorance stems partly from the very real possibility that meddling in questions concerning political prisoners is dangerous and may lead to arrest and interrogation. And it is partly due to the misleading and false propaganda disseminated by the government through the Indonesian press, radio and television.

The Government has in the past defined its attitude towards political prisoners in different ways to different audiences. At home, the Government has emphasized that the release of political prisoners was dangerous because they constituted a threat to the security of the state. Abroad, the Government has stressed the security argument and also the argument that released political prisoners would face reprisals from members of the community. Well-informed observers of Indonesia agree that these two arguments have no bearing on the question of releasing untried political prisoners; President Suharto's "New Order" has not been endangered by a serious threat of communist subversion. Moreover, the Government has not produced a single example of wide-scale reprisals against political prisoners from members of their community following their release. According to the Government's own claims, more than half a million political prisoners have been released over the last 11 years, yet it has not supplied evidence to substantiate its two lines of argument.

These questions were raised on 18 November 1976, when an Indonesian delegation visiting London requested an interview with Martin Ennals, the Secretary General of Amnesty International. The leader of the delegation, General Ali Murtopo, formerly personal adviser to President Suharto and who holds a key position in state intelligence, was asked by Martin Ennals whether in the Government's view, communist subversion was seen as a major threat, and whether there had been any wide-scale reprisals in the community against released political prisoners. General Ali Murtopo's reply was that communist subversion was not a serious threat to the Indonesian Government and that there had not been wide-scale reprisals against political prisoners.

Most recently, the Indonesian Government has abandoned its long-maintained arguments against the release of political prisoners. It now explains that further delays in the release of political prisoners are due to unemployment in Indonesia.

THE DECEMBER 1976 ANNOUNCEMENT

On 1 December 1976, the Indonesian Government announced a program for the release and/or transmigration of political prisoners. The International Commission of Jurists in Geneva, has described the prelude to this government announcement:

"During 1976, there has been intensive pressure in the US Congress and elsewhere about political detainees in Indonesia. With a view to safeguarding their foreign aid program, the Indonesian authorities have suggested that large scale releases are under way. In an interview published in the Netherlands in *De Telegraaf* on 11 June 1976, the head of the national security organisation, Admiral Sudomo, announced a plan to release the admitted 36,000 political prisoners in Indonesia, including all those on the notorious island of Buru, by the end of 1977.

"This program was received abroad with some scepticism, especially when the Foreign Minister, Adam Malik, in a statement to a US Congressional Sub-Committee made three weeks later on 30 June, contradicted Admiral Sudomo and said that the 10,000 prisoners on Buru Island would not be released but would be 'settled' there permanently. Moreover, on 24 July Admiral Sudomo stated that only 2,500 of the 34,000 category B prisoners (i.e. those against whom there is admittedly insufficient evidence to bring them to trial) would be released by the end of 1976. Finally, on 27 August 1976, Admiral Sudomo made a further announcement evading the whole issue by stating that increasing communist activities, not in Indonesia but in Malaysia and Singapore, would affect the planned release of prisoners. He said the two things which had to be taken into account were the 'possible infiltration' of communist elements from outside and the 'possible smuggling of weapons into Indonesia' to arm communist remnants there. It is shocking that tens of thousands of persons, large numbers of them having no connection with the communist party, should be kept detained without trial upon such hypothetical grounds more than 10 years after an abortive coup in which they have never been shown to have participated." (*ICJ Review* No.17, December 1976).

On 1 December 1976, the chief of staff of *Kopkamtib*, Admiral Sudomo, presided over a ceremony in Jakarta at which 2,500 category B prisoners were announced released that very day. The Government said this was the second group of category B prisoners to have been released, the first having been on 1 December 1975, totalling 1,309 persons.

Admiral Sudomo announced that: "The Government has drawn up a scheme for another phased release of the category B detainees as follows:

> 1977 — 10,000 persons
> 1978 — 10,000 persons
> 1979 — the rest."

To justify further delaying the release of category B prisoners, Admiral Sudomo said that an unspecified number of the prisoners would be "transmigrated", that is, transported to permanent penal settlements. Because "resettlement and transmigration require a large budget which could not be met in one fiscal year; hence the release by stages in 1977, 1978 and 1979".

Thus, the Indonesian Government announced a three-year plan which was apparently a scheme to release untried political prisoners, but actually meant that large numbers would be transported to permanent penal settlements, as prisoners (see Appendix II). The government's justification for transporting these prisoners to permanent penal settlements was that there were insufficient employment opportunities for the prisoners following their release, "since unemployment would create fertile ground for all kinds of acts contrary to law, and this in itself would pose a threat to the national security, particularly to law and order" (see also chapter 9).

Amnesty International finds the government's plans to "transmigrate" political prisoners to permanent penal settlements totally unacceptable. Amnesty International holds the view that all political prisoners held without trial in Indonesia, including all those already "transmigrated", should be released and should be free to return to their homes. The Indonesian Government's problem of national unemployment is not the fault of the prisoners. Political prisoners should be judged only according to the rule of law, and delay in releasing those held without trial cannot be justified by the kinds of argument offered by the Indonesian Government.

In announcing the government's December 1976 program, Admiral Sudomo said:

> "As for category A detainees, most of them have been sentenced, and the remainder will certainly be tried in our court of justice".

In this way, Admiral Sudomo has qualified a previous statement made in an interview published in the Dutch newspaper, *De Telegraaf,* on 11 June 1976. On that occasion he said that all remaining category A detainees would be tried before the end of 1979. Considering the rate at which the government has brought prisoners to trial, and the fact that the trials so far held have invariably involved a clear miscarriage of justice, there are no grounds for believing that "the remainder will certainly be tried in our court of justice" before the end of 1979. Moreover, Admiral Sudomo is mistaken in saying of the category A prisoners that "most of them have been sentenced". According to the government there are still about 1,700 category A prisoners in detention, which is much more than the 800 cases the government claims have been tried.

Admiral Sudomo also said, "As we know, detainees in category C have all been released a long time ago". As explained in Chapter 4 and contrary to what Admiral Sudomo says, local military commanders are this day announcing releases of category C prisoners and there are still category C prisoners in detention.

The Indonesian Government talks of "releases", yet declares at the same time that many prisoners will be transported to permanent penal colonies. The Government speaks of releases of all category B prisoners in a phased program over three years, recalling at the same time that, "detainees belonging to category C have all been released a long time ago". Yet, it is now known that a series of Indonesian Government assurances about alleged releases, including those given personally and repeatedly by President Suharto, were untrue and misleading.

It is Amnesty International's view that all the untried political prisoners in Indonesia should be released unconditionally and without further delay.

*   *   *

The question asked by the Indonesian journalist, Marcel Beding, in *Kompas* after his visit to Buru in December 1971 is pertinent:

> "How long have they to stay there? They themselves are asking this question. Their families are asking this question and I myself join in asking it."

APPENDIX I

THE DECISION OF THE COMMANDER OF THE *Kopkamtib*
No.KEP—028/KOPKAM/10/68 (ISSUED AND OPERATIVE
FROM 18th OCTOBER 1968) AS AMENDED BY THE
DECISION OF THE COMMANDER OF THE *Kopkamtib*
No.KEP—010/KOPKAM/3/1969 (ISSUED ON 3rd MARCH
1969 TO OPERATE RETROACTIVELY FOR THE PERIOD
SINCE 18th OCTOBER 1968)

The Commander of the Operational Command for the Restoration of
Security and Order. . .

Herewith Decides

To improve the policy of screening of civil military personnel in
Government service in the following ways:

CHAPTER 1
Article 1

This decision is an improved guide to activities concerned with purg-
ing of the civil and military personnel of Government Departments,
Bodies and Institutions of persons and elements belonging to the
treasonable G—30—S/PKI movement, including previous and subsequent activities covert and overt, so that the optimum results are
achieved, with a balanced matching of efforts and goals.

Article 2

The principles of policy contained in this decision shall provide
guidelines for acting according to the same norms in all matters of
similar character in so far as this is possible. . .

CHAPTER 2
Article 4

Those involved in the treasonable G—30—S/PKI movement are
classified as follows:

A. Those who were clearly *involved directly,* that is

1. those who planned, took part in planning or helped in the
   planning of the treasonable movement, or had foreknowledge
   of its planning and failed to report it to the authorities;

2. those who, conscious of the aims of the movement, engaged in the execution of activities within the framework of that movement, i.e.

(a) Principal Protagonists, that is persons who co-ordinated the operation and other activities;
(b) Protagonists, that is persons who implemented the actual operation or the activities mentioned in 2(a);
(c) Participants, that is persons who took part in implementing the operation and activities mentioned in 2(a).

B. Persons clearly *involved indirectly*, are

1. those who, knowing of the treasonable movement, and/or its subsequent activities, have assumed an attitude, whether by deed or word demonstrated support for this movement or opposed or hindered efforts to suppress it;
2. committee members, leaders and members of the banned PKI and/or those who had taken an oath or made promises before the PKI or before committee members or leaders of mass organizations based on the same principles as this party or operating under its aegis, together with all their activists.

C. Persons *of whom indications exist or who may reasonably be assumed to have been directly or indirectly involved*, are:

1. those who according to the existing antecedents were involved in the *Madiun* Affair* and after the September 1965 attempted coup did not clearly oppose it in any way open to them, bearing in mind their respective situations and abilities, or whose actions have always tended to support the PKI;
2. those who were members of mass organizations based on the same principles as the banned PKI or operating under its aegis;
3. those who have shown sympathy for the PKI in their attitudes and actions.

Article 5

1. Measures taken against personnel involved may be classified thus:

— Repressive actions, comprising:
a) prosecution under criminal law;
b) administrative prosecution, i.e.

(1) dishonourable dismissal;

---

* Ed — A major clash between the PKI and the Army in September 1948.

(2) restriction of opportunities in relation to certain offices and positions, due regard being paid to all regulations existing in this respect;

— Preventive actions, comprising:
1) indoctrination;
2) observation of mentality.

Article 6

The application of the several kinds of prosecutive measures shall be as follows:

1. Those classified under Article 4, letter A, shall be prosecuted under criminal law and subjected to administrative action in the form of dishonourable dismissal. While action against them is in progress they shall be kept in custody. Alternatively the Commander of the *Kopkamtib* or the Deputy Commander of the *Kopkamtib* may assign them in the interests of public order to reside in a particular place.

2. Those classified under Article 4, letter B, shall be subjected to administrative measures in the form of dishonourable dismissal. The Commander of the *Kopkamtib* or Deputy Commander of the *Kopkamtib* may assign them in the interests of security to reside in a particular place.

3. Those classified under Article 4, letter C, shall be subject to the following measures:

   a) those classified under Article 4, letter C1, shall be dismissed and placed under the supervision of the appropriate Government agencies;

   b) those classified under Article 4, letter C2, shall be subjected to restrictions in relation to particular offices and positions and shall undergo indoctrination;

   c) those classified under Article 4, letter C3, shall be placed under supervision and shall undergo indoctrination.

APPENDIX II

Embassy of the
Republic of Indonesia
Information Department

38 Grosvenor Square
London, W1
Telephone: 01-499 7661

PRESS RELEASE

No. 015/Pen/76

PRESS-STATEMENT
OF THE CHIEF OF STAFF
OF THE COMMAND FOR THE RESTORATION
OF ORDER AND SECURITY
(*Kopkamtib*)
ON DECEMBER 1, 1976

1. Today, on the 1st of December 1976, a total of 2,500 detainees involved in the PKI (Indonesian Communist Party)–September 30th Movement held at various rehabilitation institutions in Indonesia have been released, and returned to society. They were all of the "B" category detainees.

This is the second group that has been released of the above mentioned category; the first being on December 1, 1975, totalling 1,309 persons.

Those released recently consist of the following:

a) 1,430 persons from Sumatra
b) 863 persons from Java
c) 83 persons from Kalimantan
d) 80 persons from Sulawesi
e) 44 persons from Maluku.

2. In his annual state address to the Indonesian House of Representatives on August 16, 1976, President Soeharto stated that due to growing political stability coupled with the increasing stability of our national resilience, parallel to economic development the results of which are increasingly enjoyed by the people, we can now immediately solve as a whole, one of our national problems, namely that of detainees.

As we know, detainees belonging to "C" category have all been released a long time ago. Those of the "B" category, who are difficult or impossible to be brought to trial due to insufficient evidence, will have their cases speeded up hopefully after the general election next year.

Nevertheless, although their misdeeds have almost brought about the destruction of our Nation and Country, they still belong to the big family of the Indonesian Nation founded on Pancha Sila.

We must accept them back in our community. We must make them realise about their past errors, we must urge them to participate in restoring their individual life and in jointly building up the community.

In accordance with the above policy statement, the Government has drawn a scheme for another phased release of the "B" category detainees as follows:

1977 — 10,000 persons
1978 — 10,000 persons
1979 — the rest.

As for the "A" category detainees, most of them have been sentenced and the remaining will certainly be tried in our court of justice.

The main problems to be solved immediately are about the "B" category detainees:

1) There must be sufficient employment opportunities for them, since unemployment would create fertile ground for all kinds of acts contrary to law, and this in itself would pose a threat to the national security, particularly to law and order.

For this reason, the Government plans to establish transmigration centres in Sumatra, Kalimantan, Sulawesi and other places. For those who come from Java which is densely populated will be transmigrated to the island of Buru and other islands, in accordance with the guidelines on national transmigration as stated in the Second Five-Year National Development Program.

The Program states that the resettlement and transmigration require a large budget and this could not be met in one fiscal year; hence the release by phases in 1977, 1978 and 1979.

2) Those released and returned to the society will have to show concrete deeds as law abiding citizens. Their freedom as citizens is guaranteed as long as they think and act as good citizens of Indonesia based on Pancha Sila. After they are released and returned to the society, they still have to assure the Government through concrete deeds, that they consciously have discarded their

communist ideology, and that they are faithful to the Pancha Sila ideology, and as good Indonesian citizens they shall refrain from acts that are contrary to the Constitution and the Law. This adjustment is a social process in itself, which requires some time, and which also requires supervision by the society in general as well as by the law enforcement agencies.

To the society at large, I ask that everyone remains calm and unprovoked by issues created regarding the decision and program of the Government.

In fact, we should be alert and always maintain our unity for the sake of our national resilience, which is the main and decisive key in achieving our aspirations and ideals a stated in the Preambule to the 1945 Constitution which we must carry out through the one and only alternative, namely national development.

APPENDIX III(a)

Translation of relevant extracts of

DECREE OF THE PRESIDENT OF THE REPUBLIC OF INDONESIA No.11, 1963 ON ERADICATING SUBVERSIVE ACTIVITIES

THE PRESIDENT OF THE REPUBLIC OF INDONESIA,

Bearing in Mind:

a. that subversive activities are a danger to the safety and life of the people and the State which is in a state of revolution for the formation of a Socialist Indonesia;

b. that, in order to safeguard efforts to achieve the objective of the revolution, it is necessary to have a regulation to eradicate the aforesaid subversive activities;

c. that this regulation is within the framework of safeguarding the efforts to attain the objectives of the revolution so that it must be effected by means of a Presidential Decree;

DECIDES:

To enact: PRESIDENTIAL DECREE ON THE ERADICATION OF SUBVERSIVE ACTIVITIES.

CHAPTER I
SUBVERSIVE ACTIVITIES
Article 1

(1) The following shall be convicted of having engaged in subversive activities:

1. anyone who has engaged in an action with the purpose of or clearly with the purpose which is known to him or can be expected to be known to him can:

   a. distort, undermine or deviate from the ideology of the Panca Sila state or the broad policy lines of the State, or

   b. overthrow, destroy or undermine the power of the State or the authority of the lawful government or the machinery of the State, or

c. disseminate feelings of hostility or arouse hostility, cause splits, conflicts, chaos, disturbances or anxiety among the population or broad sections of society or between the State of the Republic of Indonesia and a friendly state, or

d. disturb, retard or disrupt industry, production, distribution, commerce, cooperatives or transport conducted by the Government or based upon a decision of the Government or which exerts widespread influence on the livelihood of the people.

2. any person who undertakea a deed or activity which demonstrates sympathy with an enemy of the Republic of Indonesia or with a State that is not unfriendly towards the Republic of Indonesia;

3. any person who damages or destroys installations which serve the public interest or large scale destruction of possessions, the property of individuals or organisations;

4. any person who engages in espionage activities;

5. any person who engages in sabotage.

(2) Anyone who encourages (*memikat*) such activities as referred to in paragraph (1) shall also be convicted of engaging in subversive activities.

Article 2

The following deeds to oppose the law shall be deemed to be espionage activities:

a. to possess, control or acquire any map, plan, picture or article about military buildings or military secrets or statements related to government secrets in political, diplomatic or economic affairs for the purpose of passing the same, directly or indirectly to a foreign state or organisation or to counter-revolutionaries;

b. to undertake investigations on behalf of an enemy or another State the things referred to in para (a), or to accept and receive in one's accommodation, to hide or help a person who spies on behalf of the enemy (*seorang menjelidiki musuh*);

c. to carry out, facilitate or disseminate propaganda for an enemy or for another State that is unfriendly towards the Republic of Indonesia;

d. to engage in an endeavour that conflicts with the interests of the State as a result of which a person can be investigated, guided, deprived of his freedom, or restricted, convicted or subjected to other measures by or on the authority of the enemy;

e. to give to or receive from the enemy or another State that is unfriendly towards the Republic of Indonesia or to persons assisting such an enemy or State any thing or money, or to undertake any deed that is beneficial to such an enemy or State or persons assisting it, or to endanger, obstruct or foil any measure against such an enemy or State or persons assisting it.

Article 3

The following shall be deemed to be acts of sabotage, namely deeds by a person who, with intent or clearly with intent or who knows or can be deemed to know it, in order to destroy, obstruct, retard, damage or negate something of great importance to the endeavours of the Government regarding:

a. commodities basic to the livelihood of the people, which are imported or produced by the Government;
b. production, distribution or cooperatives which are under control of the Government;
c. military, industrial, production and State commercial projects;
d. general construction projects related to industry, production, distribution and communications;
e. State installations;
f. communications (land, sea, air and telecommunications).

CHAPTER II
INVESTIGATION AND CONVICTION OF
SUBVERSIVE ACTIVITIES
Article 4

All departments of State are to assist in investigating subversive activities.

CHAPTER IV
PUNISHMENT
Article 13

(1) Any person who commits acts of subversion as specified in Article 1, paragraph 1, numbers 1, 2, 3, 4 and paragraph 2 shall be sentenced to death, to life imprisonment or to a prison sentence of a maximum of 20 (twenty) years.

(2) Any person who commits acts of subversion as specified in Article 1, paragraph 1, number 5 shall be sentenced to death, to life imprisonment or to a prison sentence of a maximum of 20 (twenty) years and/or a fine of at the most 30 (thirty) million rupiahs.

Article 14

All goods whether the property or not the property of the convicted person which have been acquired as a result of, or which have been used in the implementation of the acts of subversion can be confiscated.

APPENDIX III(b)

Defence Plea of Oei Tju Tat   3 March, 1976

IMPLEMENT TRISAKTI, THE CROWNING GLORY OF
REAL INDEPENDENCE

Trisakti 1. Sovereignty in political affairs.
2. Self-reliance in economic affairs.
3. Distinctive identity in cultural affairs.

1. Members of the Court,

First permit me, through this session, to express my appreciation and thanks to all groups and people who have at all times given me their attention, and sympathy and shown confidence in me, each in their own way. These people include pastors, priests and nuns, many of whom I do not personally know, also friends, acquaintances, comrades in struggle who are still behind barbed wire or who are out there in society, colleagues and lawyers at home and abroad, not forgetting Adnan Buyung Nasution, Amnesty International and other international organisations active in the defence of human rights, the International Commission of Jurists, Pax Christi, some members of the British House of Lords, and certain officials who, directly or indirectly helped to arrange this trial, including some state officials, some of whom occupy senior and the highest posts.

I should also like to express my appreciation of the wisdom of the Court of Judges in guiding these hearings.

Finally my boundless thanks to the team of lawyers, Mr Yap Thiam Hien, Mr Djamaluddin Datuk Singo Mangkuto and Mr Albert Hasibuan, who have given so much time and expertise, being inspired by the desire to serve truth and justice, and to help the struggle to uphold the rule of law in this Panca Sila State. My deepest gratitude to them for doing all this *con amore*.

2. As regards this so-called case of mine, is it really true that I infringed the law? Or are there political reasons that, whatever the outcome of the case, I must be set aside from society, if necessary by means of a new version of the Dreyfus Affair, a kind of van de Lubbe case or Multatuli's "he-must-hang" case?

It is a fact that although I was arrested in March 1966 it was not until three years later, in about the middle of 1969, that I was interrogated. Then there were three more years of nothing; I was never asked anything. Then in 1972, I was interrogated again, not as a continuation of the 1969 interrogations but just a repeat interrogation about the same things. Goodness only knows how many times altogether interrogations were carried out; so much so, that one officer, CPM Colonel Noordali let slip, that many of the charges against me were nothing more than slanders. It became difficult to conceal the fact that my 'case' was being treated like a pingpong ball between the compentent authorities. So, it is easy to understand that, even though it was announced in April 1974, my so-called case would "very soon" be brought to trial, it was subsequently repeatedly announced that it was being postponed for various reasons. Once it was reported that a committee had been set up to study this case, and . . . heaven knows with what result. But later, new people were appointed to handle the 'case' and it was even said that the initial documents of the *Teperpu* Team (Central Interrogation Team) had been lost. . .!

And then, a high-level State official actually discussed it with the most senior State official and two of his colleagues. All said indeed that there was certainly no case to answer.

All this, together with the fact that I am present in this court today provided an answer to the above mentioned question. There has clearly been a process of pull and push. Those who can see no reason preferring charges against me, have lost, while those wanting a political trial rather than a legal trial have won, for the time being, as is obvious from the Prosecution's *Requisitoire* *.

3. I still strongly deny all the charges made against me. The legal aspects will be dealt with by my defence lawyers. By even a superficial study of my demeanor, origin, background, life-style, environment and family, people would not easily conclude that I would be likely to engage in subversive activities. What is more, if my political opinions and interests are taken into account, this would make such a charge even less likely. Just imagine "subverting the legal government at that time". Is it not a fact, according to the 1945 Constitution which is official and lawful to this very day, that the legitimate government at that time was non other than the Government of President Sukarno. So what does this make me?

---

* *Requisitoire:* In Indonesian legal practices it is the demand made by the public prosecutor for the punishment of the accused in the charges stated.

In the book *From Private to President* by a German journalist G. Roder which is a biography of General Suharto, it says that President Suharto mentioned me as a comrade in Sukarno's struggle. Who then would not be astonished and at the same time amused to hear that I, reputedly as a fellow traveller of Sukarno am accused of subversion against the Sukarno Government of which I myself was a member! Is the purpose here to discredit Sukarno of whom I was a follower? This too, is quite absurd.

4. These court hearings are open to the public, in accordance with the basic principles of justice. It is therefore certain that the things said in this courtroom will be heard not only in various parts of the country but also beyond the borders of Indonesia. In short, the whole world will be in a position to judge the extent to which truth, justice and adherence to the law are valid in this Panca Sila State.

So, it is correct and proper for all those playing a part in this trial to endeavour to ensure that it is a fair trial for the sake of the good name of the State and Government of Indonesia because it will be impossible to conceal any of this from the eyes and ears of people abroad.

How disappointed and amazed I was to hear the Prosecutor's *requisitoire* delivered on 25 February 1976. I think the Court will agree that a *requisitoire* should be a resumé of the results of the Court hearings and not the fantasies which the Prosecuting Counsel had in his mind before this trial started. I am therefore quite amazed that this *requisitoire* completely ignores matters that came to light during the hearings, and in places even made points that completely contradict what had been said in court. I shall give just a few examples, as there are too many to mention them all:

(a) I never said that the 4 October 1965 Partindo C. Board statement was the result of the meeting that was held at my home, Jalan Blitar, 10;

(b) It is not true that witness Armunanto said that the statement was the unanimous decision reached by the Partindo C.B. at its meeting on 3 October 1965.

(c) It is not true that witness H. Winoto Danuasmoro said that I was among the persons who had made the 4 October statement, etc, etc.

It is really difficult to understand why the Prosecution failed to hear things said in these hearings, for instance:

(i) the categorical statements by witnesses Armunanto, Adisumarto and Sutomo that I did not participate in the discussion although they were held at Jalan Blitar 10, that no decision was taken at my home because we still had to await the results of the discussion between the three Partindo Ministers and President Sukarno in Bogor.

(ii) the statements made by all these witnesses plus witnesses Winoto Danuasmoro and Sardjono that it was initially I who made objections to the said 4 October Partindo statement, etc, etc.

5. Members of the Court, it would be tedious to repeat everything that has been said by various witnesses during these hearings. Happily we live in this electronic age, so that tapes taken of all the proceedings make it impossible for us to imagine things or hear only what we want to hear. My summary of the hearings, which can if necessary be checked against the tapes, is:

a) *Re the 4 October Partindo Statement*

All witnesses confirmed that I did not participate in the discussions held in my home on 3 October 1965; that the 4 October statement was drafted by other persons or persons in another place without awaiting the results of the meeting of the three Partindo ministers and President Sukarno in Bogor; that I rejected the statement because the coup conspirators had dismissed the Dwikora Cabinet which for me meant that it was a coup d'etat attempt and that therefore it was not a matter of concern only to the Army but had a nationwide scope. Moreover, I had already committed myself in my letter to the President/Supreme Commander/Great Leader of the Revolution, Sukarno and Deputy Prime Minister Dr J. Leimena on 2 October 1965, and that therefore I was the first person to protest at the 4 October statement.

One further comment about all this: it is ridiculous indeed that I as a member of the Fact Finding Commission never before heard in the regions anything about the dissemination of that statement or the consequences of that statement. What the Commission did know was that victims of the murders, robberies and other things were members of the Nadhlatul Ulama, the PKI and the Partai Nasional Indonesia, and the majority were non-party people, so that the construction made in the *requisitoire* about the effects of that statement are really too far-fetched.

b) *Re my remarks at the Baperki Xth Anniversary and the East Java Provincial Partindo Committee Meeting*

Presumably the Court will be able to draw its own conclusions from the testimony of several witnesses which certainly did not make any sense; for instance the call for the formation of a Disaster Victims Aid Committee, about the nominations for East Java Governor etc. My statements were all basically the same, and it was all just a matter of routine. Further, it should be noted that the demonstrations were organised or sponsored by the various Fronts that existed: The Youth Front, the National Front, etcetera. Thus it was quite impossible for Partindo, let alone me, to play about with instructions.

c) *Re the so-called information from Junta Suardi*

The witness himself expressed doubts about the truth of this information which meant that he himself did not come to my office but thought it enough to send a copy of it via his assistant on 25 September 1965. But the important thing is that I had just returned home from abroad on 23 September. Quite candidly, if indeed I had been able to receive that letter the next day, the first thing I would certainly have done would have been to have called Junta Suardi and checked its reliability before reporting to the President. The fact is that the first time I heard about this question was at my interrogation in 1969 at Nirabaya Camp, by Lieutenant-Colonel Tatang.

d) *Re my briefing at the Partindo C.Board Meeting*

As regards the things mentioned by witnesses Ismail Ishak and Moh Noor Nasution about an "executive meeting of the Partindo C. Board" on a Friday in August 1965 which, so they say, was attended by Asmara Hadi, Winoto Danuasmoro, Armunanto, K. Werdoyo Sardjono and others, and on which occasion I was said to have given a briefing about President Sukarno's illness and so on, this has been proven false by the testimony of the witnesses themselves as well as by sheer common sense. Such a meeting could not logically have taken place after 17 August 1965, when President Sukarno appeared in public in excellent health and delivered his independence day speech; whereas on the Fridays just before 17 August 1965, those persons named as having attended the meeting, including me, were not in Jakarta.

e) *Re demonstrations*

Witness Achmad Johar, deputy of the demonstration against USIS Jakarta stated that the demonstration was reported to the Minister/Secretary General of the National Front who, after consulting with the four commanders of the Armed Forces, reached the decision that a number of USIS books would be "detained" at Salemba Prison. Nothing was destroyed, and the demonstration was controlled jointly by the Youth Front and the police. I do not know about any delegates coming to my office. I personally have no objection to demonstrations because in those days there was no ban on demonstrations. Demonstrations were permitted by the government, which subsequently halted all USIS activities in Indonesia.

Some of those who now feel that their feet were trodden on during demonstrations in those days—in Jakarta, as well as in Surabaya and elsewhere and who now wish to attribute all the responsibility to me would do well to read *The Impossible Dream* by Howard Jones, former US Ambassador in Jakarta, who carefully recorded everything. He of all people represented those directly concerned and he makes no wild allegations as some people do these days. This shows the groundlessness of all these false charges about my inciting people in Surabaya.

6. Members of the Court, certain points need to be made:

a) The Prosecuting Counsel considers that I committed subversion. Common sense would suggest that the person competent to judge whether or not I committed subversion was the late President Sukarno or at the very least the Cabinet Presidium to which I had been seconded; or, members of that former Cabinet. It is therefore most regrettable that Dr Subandrio, Dr J. Leimena, Foreign Minister Adam Malik and Rev. J.W. Rumambi were not permitted to testify in these hearings.

One thing is clear—that President Sukarno in several Cabinet reshuffles before and after the attempted coup retained me in his Cabinet. And even after a slander campaign had started against me, President Sukarno, in the Cabinet Session on 6 November 1965, defended me.

It has been reported that according to investigations by a US Senate Committee, the late President Sukarno was a target of CIA activity, so one should look in that direction if one is looking for acts of subversion during the Sukarno Government's period of office. It is tragic that only now, after President Sukarno has been dead for 6 years and when I no longer sit in the government but have spent the past ten years behind barbed wire, other people or groups now want to pass judgement on me.

b) This also applies to the opinion that I attach more importance to party interests than to my position as Minister of State. If this were true, I would certainly not be standing here before this court. But that view has proved false, and in previous sessions dissatisfied voices were heard, complaining that I did not have the powers to place people from my own party in jobs in my secretariat; I was called arrogant, a know-all and not prepared to listen to the party, etc. It is significant that among the witnesses brought to these hearings by the Prosecution there has not been a single person from the Armed Forces, the government or persons of civil rank, but they were all from Partindo. This strongly suggests that this 'case' has exploited the personal sentiments and weaknesses of some Partindo members, and that therefore it is not altogether businesslike.

c) I should like to express my appreciation to the Prosecutor for still acknowledging in his *requisitoire* that I am a nationalist, within the NAS grouping (of NASAKOM). Indeed, if I were a communist, why beat about the bush and not admit it? We should not close our eyes to the facts of history that communist ideology and power are becoming more significant in world politics. Nor can we ignore the fact that the Indonesian communist movement contributed to the nation's struggle for independence from Dutch colonialism, from Japanese fascism, as well as opposing imperialism, colonialism and neo-colonialism in the years following 1945.

But I hereby declare that I, in my entire existence, have never been able to accept the ideology and political doctrine of communism in particular its materialist philosophy and certain communist practices. Neither have I ever been a communist sympathiser nor been used by them. Were what the Prosecution says true—that I once co-operated with the PKI or with PKI people, so long as the PKI or these other people did not jeopardise the political interests of President Sukarno or Partindo, why should I refuse to collaborate with them in the same way as I collaborated in the past with other political groups? Nor should it be forgotten that there were (or at the least there were attempts) towards cooperation between nine political parties that were legal at that time, right up to the outbreak of the contemptible G.30.s movement.

The well-known statesman, Averill Harriman who was once US Assistant Secretary of State for Eastern Affairs said in a TV interview when asked about Sukarno: "He is not a communist. He is a nationalist." Let us hope that people in Indonesia can distinguish between progressive nationalists, socialist nationalists (read *Achieving Independent Indonesia* by Sukarno) and communists.

d) As regards condemning the coup conspirators, (see page 23 of the Prosecuting Counsel's *requisitoire*), I hope the Prosecution contacts the Department of Trade and that it will still find there a tape of a meeting between the Minister of Trade, Brigadier-General A. Jusuf and some leading businessmen from the capital, held in the days following the coup affair. At the request of Minister Jusuf, I was present at that meeting. It was there that for the very first time, a state official categorically described the attempted coup as a "deplorable national tragedy". And that person was the one who is now standing before you all.

(The juridical aspects of the defence to be handled by the Defence Team. The remainder is a summary of Oei's political views.)

APPENDIX IV

PRISONERS ON BURU: SOME CASE HISTORIES

When the Indonesian Government began to transport prisoners to Buru in 1969, they promised that the men sent there would be fit adults, chosen after medical examination. But it became clear later that the selection of prisoners was done without much regard for the Government's declared basis of selection. One cause for serious concern is the fact that about 600 of the detainees now imprisoned on Buru were youths under 21 when they were transported to the island.

Most of the prisoners in the penal camps on Buru are ordinary Indonesians—labourers, office workers, town workers in various occupations. Little is known about these people individually. Also on Buru are a number of distinguished Indonesian intellectuals, who were associated with left-wing organizations, some of which were affiliated to the Indonesian Communist Party when that party was legally playing an active part in Indonesian politics before 1965. (Intellectuals—Pramoedya Aranta Tur and Karel Supit.)
The following is a representative selection of prisoners on Buru.

Soehadi

Soehadi is a farmer, of about 34, from Central Java. The precise circumstances of his arrest are not known, but he has been in detention since 1965. He has not heard from his family since he was arrested. His mother now lives with his sister. His father died many years ago.

Rivai Apin

Rivai Apin, a well-known writer and poet, was born in 1927 in Minangkabau, Central Sumatra. He was a founder member in 1946 of *Gelanggang,* a cultural organization whose aim it was to encourage Indonesian writing based on the principles of humanism and internationalism. Before Indonesia's independence in 1945 most intellectuals used Dutch as their first language; consequently little was written in Indonesian. It was only during the independence struggle against the Dutch that a group of Indonesian nationalist writers appeared.

Apin became active in LEKRA, the left-wing cultural association, during the mid-1950s, and in 1956, he became editor of *Zaman Baru,* a PKI supported journal. In 1959, he was elected to the Executive Committee of LEKRA.

Precise details about the circumstances of Apin's arrest are not known, but he was most probably detained at the end of 1965.

Soedono

Soedono, a painter and decorator, was arrested in 1968 and detained in Jakarta before being transport' ˜ to Buru some time between 1969 and 1971. He was a member of LEKRA. Soedono was born in 1933 in Java; his wife and five children still live in Jakarta.

Asmudji

Asmudji, aged about 43, is a former teacher. He was active in left-wing political affairs from his early youth and belonged to the youth organization *Pesindo,* which subsequently became *Pemuda Rakyat.* He was also a member of the *Pemuda Rakyat* Central Board. Asmudji was arrested in 1965, and first detained in Salemba Prison in Jakarta. In 1969, he was transported to Buru Island. His wife Suning was arrested with him, and has been detained since then in Bukit Duri Prison, Jakarta.

Purwadi

Purwadi, aged 33, graduated from the Economic Secondary School, and was a member of *Penuda Rakyat,* the youth organization banned in 1966. At the time of his arrest in December 1965, he was working in the Madukismo Sugar Factory. Purwadi is one of about 200 detainees on Buru whose families have come to join them in prison, despite the unsatisfactory conditions.

Tjoo Tik Tjoon

Tjoo Tik Tjoon, aged 55, was a member of parliament representing the Indonesian Communist Party from 1956 to 1963. He also belonged to BAPERKI, The Consultative Body of Indonesian Citizenship, founded in 1954 in order to secure full civil and human rights for all Indonesian citizens, particularly racial minorities and especially the Chinese. Mr Tjoo was arrested on 24 December 1965, and first detained in army barracks in Jakarta. He was subsequently moved to a prison outside Jakarta, and in 1961 transported to Buru. His wife and some of his children are still in Jakarta.

Sumardjo

Sumardjo is one of several hundred boys who were arrested when teenagers and who now face indefinite detention on Buru. At the time of his arrest, Sumardjo was in the second year of senior high school and a member of *Ikatan Pemuda Paladjar Indonesia,* the League of High School Students, a left-wing students' organization. Precise details about Sumardjo's arrest are not known, but he was probably in his mid-teens at that time, and is now only about 25.

Basuki Effendi

Basuki Effendi is one of Indonesia's foremost film directors, a number of whose films have received international awards. He is about 43, is married and has two children. He was a member of the film section of LEKRA, and in 1959, was elected on to its Central Executive. He was first arrested in October 1965 and detained for four months in Jakarta. After his release in February 1966, he was unable to return to his former work. He was re-arrested in 1969 and transported to Buru in 1971.

Ferdinand Runturambi

Ferdinand Runturambi is a former member of parliament and active trade unionist. He was born in Sumatra in November 1918, and is a practising Roman Catholic. He became involved in the labour movement while working as an official in the Ministry of Public Works and Energy in 1950, and in 1953 was elected on to the Central Bureau of SOBSI, the trade union federation. Two years later, in 1955, he was elected on to its National Council, and finally, in 1964, he became third Deputy Chairman of SOBSI. Runturambi was also active in the international labour movement and attended the Moscow International Economic Conference in 1952 and the World Federation of Trade Unions meetings in Bandung and Colombo in 1954, where he became an alternate member of the General Council.

Runturambi was an active supporter of the Indonesian independence movement. In 1945, he was arrested by the Japanese because of his work in the nationalist movement and detained for a short period.

Iskander Sukarno

Iskander Sukarno, aged about 48, was a member of the Indonesian Communist Party. He was employed by the Department of Education as an inspector of secondary schools in Jakarta until 1965. He was first arrested in 1965, but released early in 1966. He was re-arrested in October 1968, detained at first in Salemba Prison, Jakarta, and later moved to a prison camp in Nusakembangan. In 1976, he was one ι ι the first detainees to be transported to Buru since 1971, when transportation stopped after the first 10,000 prisoners were established there. Although his wife was able to visit him in Nusakembangan in south-central Java, communication with him is now almost impossible.

Tom Anwar

Tom Anwar was Deputy Chief Editor of the newspaper *Bintang Timur* and a member of the Indonesian Journalists' Association. He was arrested in late 1965 and was one of the first prisoners to be transported to Buru in 1969. He is aged about 50, married and has several children.

Tjiptoharsojo

Tjiptoharsojo was a teacher in Bondowoso, East Java and a member of a radical teachers' association. After the attempted coup in October 1965, he and his wife, also a teacher, fled from Bondowoso to Surabaya and then to Jakarta, where Tjiptoharsojo was finally arrested in 1968. His wife, afraid to leave her husband alone, accompanied him to the office of the unit that arrested him, where she too was arrested and detained for five years. After her release in 1974, she was forced to find accommodation in Army barracks in Jakarta, as she had nowhere to live. Tjiptoharsojo was transported to Buru some time after 1969. In the four years since then his wife has received only two letters from him.

Richard Paingot Situmeang

Richard Paingot Situmeang was born in Tarutung, Sumatra in 1919. He is a Christian, a former member of parliament, elected in 1955, and a leading trade unionist. In 1937, he began working in the oil fields in Sumatra, where he helped organize the nationalist movement among his fellow workers during the Japanese occupation and where he helped form a union of young oil workers. He also belonged to the Indonesian Socialist Youth organization, *Pesindo*. In 1951, he was elected on to the Central Executive Committee of SOBSI, the trade union federation, and in 1960 on to its national presidium. Because of his leading position in SOBSI, he travelled extensively outside Indonesia attending conferences in a number of places, including Peking and Vienna. He was arrested in late 1965 with his wife, who was released in the early 1970s. They have eight children.

* * *

The well-known Indian poet and journalist Dom Moraes visited Buru in 1972 and reported on the plight of the prisoners in the *Asia Magazine* and in the London *Daily Telegraph* (24 March 1972):

"It was stupid, in 1965, to decide that a mass of small, helpless people, clerks and bank tellers and office workers, were all hardline communists: stupid to decide that several of the leading intellectuals of the country were hardline communists without any trial or investigation whatever. It is stupid to have kept them locked up for six years, unable to communicate with their families, and eventually committed them to Buru, 2,000 miles from their homes. It is stupid to try and turn intellectuals into manual labourers."

APPENDIX V

EXTRACTS FROM MEMORANDUM TO PRESIDENT SUHARTO AND THE GOVERNMENT OF INDONESIA SUBMITTED BY THE CHAIRMAN OF AMNESTY INTERNATIONAL
(February 1971)

While fully appreciating the extremely difficult and dangerous situation which faced the Indonesian Government in 1965 and 1966, it is considered that the continued detention of vast numbers of persons who are uncharged and untried clearly contravenes the provisions of the Universal Declaration of Human Rights and the norms of the Rule of Law. The continuance of this situation is obviously highly damaging to the image of Indonesia in the outside world; it also tends to prolong the memory and bitterness resulting from the tragic events of 1965. From discussions we have had with both the responsible civil and military authorities in Jakarta, we believe that the Indonesian Government appreciates the necessity of dealing with this problem.

"One of the difficulties we have found in the course of our investigations is the absence of reliable public statistics as to the number of prisoners held. . .

". . .It is strongly recommended that the Government should take steps to obtain and publish precise figures as to the numbers held. Unless this is done the Government itself and the international agencies which are prepared to help the Government will be faced with added difficulties in the formulation of release programs.

"In regard to the Category A prisoners the problem as we see it is that even if charges and evidence are available to put them on trial, the existing judicial machinery is totally inadequate to undertake the trial of 5,000 persons. It is understood that it is the intention of the Government to appoint five hundred new judges by 1974 for the purpose of undertaking these trials. Even if the Government does find it possible to appoint five hundred new judges and the necessary ancillary legal personnel within the course of the next two or three years, the trial of some 5,000 persons is bound to take another 10 years or so. This would mean that many of those awaiting trial will probably die before they are tried and that in a number of cases trials will take place only some 10 to 15 years after the events that form the basis of charges. This is obviously most unsatisfactory. It is therefore suggested that a re-assessment of the cases of the 5,000 prisoners in Category A should be undertaken with a view to the release of those against whom there is no evidence and of those who even if guilty of some offence, could be regarded as having purged their offence by the 5 years they have already spent in prison. It is believed that if such a review of the Category A prisoners were undertaken, the number remaining for trial would be considerably reduced. The program for the strengthening of the judicial machinery and the appointment of additional judges should in any case be proceeded with as the existing judicial machinery is insufficient by any standards. The existing judges, while dedicated, are overwhelmed with work.

"In regard to the Category B prisoners it is suggested that in these cases too there should be a complete revaluation. It is completely contrary to the norms of the Rule of Law that persons suspected of being 'communist' should be detained indefinitely without charge or trial. If any of them are alleged to have committed crimes, they should be tried. . .

"The principal reason advanced by members of the Government for the slowness in the release of the Category C prisoners is the fear of physical reprisals by the local populations. There has been no evidence of such an attitude by the population in the very substantial releases which have taken place in the last year. It is confidently hoped that the President and members of the Government could offset any such danger by appealing to the population to facilitate the reintegration of the released prisoners into the life of the Indonesian nation.

"Without questioning the well-meaning motives which may have inspired the massive transportation of untried prisoners to island detention camps, it is a policy which is fraught with grave danger and which cannot be justified under any legal concept. The transportation for life of 10,000 prisoners, mostly males, without their families to camps on remote islands is clearly contrary to the laws of humanity and to justice. What is to happen to these vast penal settlements in the future? Is this the best way of eradicating the bitterness and dissension of the past? Is it wise to create substantial pockets of population, which will not unnaturally nourish resentment against the authorities who have transported them there? If any program of resettlement for ex-prisoners is envisaged, this should be done on the basis of reintegration of the ex-prisoners into the life of the community and wherever possible, on the basis of family grouping. . .

"In relation to the treatment of all prisoners we would respectfully draw the attention of the Indonesian Government to the provisions of the United Nations Standard Minimum Rules for the Treatment of Prisoners. We appreciate that in the existing circumstances it will take some time before they can be fully put into operation in Indonesia. We would, however, urge that copies of these Rules should be supplied to the commandants of all military camps of detention where prisoners are detained.

"The concern of Amnesty International in making the propositions herein set forth was to put forward proposals which might be of assistance to the Indonesian Government in the solution of a problem which is of paramount importance for the future development and stability of the Republic of Indonesia. Amnesty International and indeed the other international organisations working in the human rights field would, we feel, be more than willing to extend any assistance in their power to the Indonesian Government to secure the constructive solution of these problems".

APPENDIX VI

AMNESTY INTERNATIONAL ACTIONS ON BEHALF OF INDONESIAN POLITICAL PRISONERS

From its founding in 1961, Amnesty International has taken up cases of Indonesian political prisoners detained without trail by the former administration of the late President Sukarno. Thus, for example, the distinguished Indonesian journalist Mochtar Lubis, who was imprisoned without trial for more than nine years in all by President Sukarno, was adopted by Amnesty International as a prisoner of conscience. When in 1975, Mr Lubis was imprisoned by President Suharto's Government, Amnesty International again adopted.

Since 1965, the focus of Amnesty International's work for Indonesian political prisoners has been an adoption program which over the years has led to the taking up of the cases of hundreds of prisoners who were known not to have been personally involved in the abortive coup of 1965. Amnesty International adoption groups in many countries have written to the Indonesian Government urging the release of the prisoners.

In addition, the organization provided information about Indonesian political prisoners. In February 1973, Amnesty International made a submission to the Secretary General of the United Nations asking the UN Commission on Human Rights to "intercede with the Government of Indonesia to ensure the immediate trial or release of all untried prisoners". Evidence was presented to show that the government's policy "revealed a consistent pattern of gross violations of human rights and fundamental freedoms".

In March 1973, a documented and illustrated report, *Indonesia Special,* was published jointly by the International Secretariat and the Dutch Section of Amnesty International. In it Sean MacBride, then Chairman of Amnesty International, appealed to President Suharto and the Indonesian Government to announce a general amnesty for all untried prisoners (see Appendix 5).

For several years, the organization's International Secretariat has sent information about Indonesian political prisoners to governments of all countries who belong to the Inter-Governmental Group on Indonesia (the international consortium of governments giving aid to Indonesia) drawing their attention to the situation of political prisoners.

The Indonesian Government's attitude to Amnesty International has been ambivalent. The first Amnesty International mission to Indonesia was by Professor Julius Stone, a distinguished international lawyer from Australia, in July 1969. This was followed by a second mission, by Sean MacBride, then Secretary General of the International Commission of Jurists and later, in October 1970, Chairman of Amnesty International. In July 1972, a mission by Professor Telford Taylor of Columbia University, New York, and Professor James Harrison, then Chairman of Amnesty International, United States Section, had to be cancelled when the latter's visa application was refused. In January 1975, an Amnesty International delegation from Australia, led by Mr Richard McGarvie, Chairman of the Victoria Bar Council and now a Supreme Court Judge, went to Jakarta, but Indonesian ministers and officials who were directly concerned with political imprisonment refused, or said they were unable to meet the delegation to discuss the problem of imprisonment.

For many years, Amnesty International has criticized government policies which have adversely affected political prisoners. The particularly desperate circumstances of women prisoners was publicized in an international campaign in April 1975, focussed on Kartini Day, which is celebrated in Indonesia as Women's Day to commemorate the famous national heroine. During International Women's Year, Indonesia stood out as the country with probably the largest number of women political prisoners.

Amnesty International sections undertook campaigns on Indonesian Independence Day, 17 August 1975. The organization's Swedish Section collected the signatures of 130 parliamentarians on a petition for the release of untried political prisoners. In the Federal Republic of Germany, about 31,000 signatures were collected. In Austria, also several thousand signatures were collected, and in all three countries, the petitions were delivered to the Indonesian Embassy.

In October 1975, a coordinated international campaign took up the cases of the tens of thousands of prisoners who had by then spent up to 10 years in detention without trial. Publicity was organized at local, national and international levels. Many Amnesty International adoption groups publicized the situation in their own local communities, by means of information stalls, discussion groups and articles in the local press. In the United States, Australia, the Netherlands, Austria, Canada and other countries, there was extensive coverage by press, radio and television.

In April 1976, there was another Amnesty International campaign on behalf of women prisoners. Many national sections, Nigerian, Japanese, Belgian and Swiss sent appeals and petitions to the Indonesian Government for the release of the women prisoners.

In autumn 1976, a major Amnesty International campaign publicized the organization's criticism of the Indonesian Government's Buru "transmigration" program. There was wide news coverage in many countries, including the United States, Canada, France, the Netherlands and Australia.

This publication coincides with the beginning of a major international campaign to inform people all over the world about the plight of the tens of thousands of political prisoners in Indonesia. Information about this campaign is available from the appropriate national sections of Amnesty International, or from the International Secretariat in London.

AMNESTY INTERNATIONAL PUBLICATIONS

Report on Allegations of Torture in Brazil, A5, 108 pages, first edition September 1972, re-set with updated preface March 1976: £1.20 (US $3.00).

A Chronicle of Current Events (Journal of the Human Rights Movement in the USSR), numbers 17, 18, 21, 24, 27 published individually: 65 pence (US $1.60); double volumes 19—20, 22—23, 25—26: 85 pence (US $2.10); numbers 28—31 in one volume: 95 pence (US $2.50); numbers 32—33, one volume, £1.95 (US $4.95).

Chile: an Amnesty International Report, A5, 80 pages in English, 88 pages Spanish, September 1974: 85 pence (US $2.10).

Report on an Amnesty International Mission to Spain, A5, 24 pages in English, 28 pages Spanish, September 1975: 35 pence (US $0.90).

Prisoners of Conscience in the USSR: Their Treatment and Conditions, A5, 154 pages, November 1975: £1.00 (US $2.50).

AI in Quotes, A5, 24 pages, May 1976: 25 pence (US $0.50).

Amnesty International 1961—1976: A chronology, May 1976: 20 pence (US $0.40).

Professional Codes of Ethics, A5, 32 pages, October 1976: 40 pence (US $1.00). Also available in Spanish.

Report of an Amnesty International Mission to Sri Lanka, A4, 52 pages, second edition December 1976: 75 pence (US $1.25).

Los Abogados Contra La Tortura, A4, 31 pages, first published in Spanish, January 1977: 60 pesetas, 50 pence (US $1.00).

Report of an Amnesty International Mission to the Republic of the Philippines, A5, 60 pages, first published September 1976, second (updated) edition March 1977: £1.00. Also available in Spanish.

Dossier on political prisoners held in secret detention camps in Chile, A4, March 1977: £1.45. Also available in Spanish.

Report of an Amnesty International Mission to Argentina, A4, 92 pages, March 1977: £1.00. Also available in Spanish.

Torture in Greece: The First Torturers' Trial 1975, A5, 98 pages, April 1977: 85 pence.

Islamic Republic of Pakistan. An Amnesty International Report including the findings of a Mission, A4, 96 pages, May 1977: 75 pence.

Evidence of Torture: Studies by the Amnesty International Danish Medical Group, A5, 40 pages, June 1977: 50 pence.

Report of an Amnesty International Mission to The Republic of Korea, A4, 46 pages, first published April 1976 second edition June 1977: 75 pence.

The Republic of Nicaragua. An Amnesty International Report including the findings of a Mission to Nicaragua 10—15 May 1976, A4, 75 pages, July 1977: 75 pence.

In addition to these major reports, Amnesty International also publishes a monthly Newsletter, an Annual Report and a regular series of Amnesty International Briefing Papers:

Amnesty International Briefing Papers: a new series of human rights reference booklets on individual countries, averaging between 12—16 pages in A5 format. Briefing Papers Number 1—11:

Singapore	Rhodesia/Zimbabwe	People's Democratic
Paraguay*	Malawi	Republic of Yemen
Iran	Guatemala*	Taiwan (Republic of China)
Namibia	Turkey	Czechoslovakia*

* also available in Spanish

Subscription price for series of 10 briefing papers: £6.00 (US $15). Price includes postage and packing. Single copies 40 pence (US $1.00), plus 20 pence (50 cents) for postage and handling.

Amnesty International Newsletter and Annual Report: The Newsletter is a six-page monthly account of Amnesty International's work for human rights in countries throughout the world and includes a two-page bulletin on the work of the Campaign for the Abolition of Torture. The Annual Report gives a country-by-country survey of human rights violations which have come to the attention of Amnesty International. Yearly subscription £6.00 (US $15.00) inclusive.

Amnesty International Publications are available in English and in most cases have been translated into other major world languages by the International Secretariat or by the national sections of Amnesty International.

Copies of Amnesty International Publications can be obtained from the offices of the national sections of Amnesty International. Office addresses and further information may be obtained from the International Secretariat, 10 Southampton Street, London WC2E 7HF, England.